Madame De La Fayette, Thomas Sergeant Perry

The Princess of Cleves

Vol. I

Madame De La Fayette, Thomas Sergeant Perry

The Princess of Cleves
Vol. I

ISBN/EAN: 9783337129330

Printed in Europe, USA, Canada, Australia, Japan

Cover: Foto ©ninafisch / pixelio.de

More available books at **www.hansebooks.com**

MADAME DE LAFAYETTE

THE
PRINCESS OF CLÈVES.

BY

MADAME DE LA FAYETTE.

TRANSLATED BY

THOMAS SERGEANT PERRY.

WITH ILLUSTRATIONS DRAWN BY JULES GARNIER, AND
ENGRAVED BY A. LAMOTTE.

IN TWO VOLUMES.

VOL. I.

BOSTON:
LITTLE, BROWN, AND COMPANY.
1891.

CONTENTS TO VOL. I.

	PAGE
PREFACE	7
PART I.	47
PART II.	131

PREFACE.

THE "PRINCESS OF CLÈVES" was published in the spring of 1678 by Claude Barbin, whose place of business was on the second floor of the Sainte-Chapelle. It was a good house, for Barbin was the publisher of Boileau, La Fontaine, and Racine. The "Phèdre" had appeared but a short time before; the first volume of a new edition of the "Fables" had just been put on sale; and for the autumn there was announced a fifth edition, much enlarged, of the "Maxims" of Monsieur de la Rochefoucauld. Barbin was no Elzevir; he wrought, not for students or for connoisseurs, but for the court and the town. His books were printed without elegance, and were designed for a wide circulation. He had shrewdly printed the "Princess of Clèves" in four small volumes, in large type,—doubtless in order to be able to ask the highest possible price for a book long announced and belauded; possibly, too, in order that ladies might be able to carry into bowers and drawing-rooms the light volumes of a book written for them by one of themselves.

The "Princess of Clèves" bore no author's name. Etiquette forbade that there should be exposed on the stalls of the Palais and of the Rue Saint-Jacques the titlepage of a book bearing the name of a lady of the court. It was commonly supposed that the Duke of

La Rochefoucauld, the lover of Madame de la Fayette, had lent his aid, and that perhaps Segrais had written part of it.[1] Segrais, a poor gentleman and an academician, had for some time been a member of the household of Madame de la Fayette, occupying an humble position in an elegant and noble domesticity. In 1670 he had put his name to "Zaïde: a Spanish Story," which Monsieur Huet and all the duke's friends freely attributed to Madame de

---

[1] There was published this introductory note, from "The Publisher to the Reader," which denied nothing, confessed nothing, and contained an unfulfilled promise: "In spite of the approval that readers have expressed for this story, the author has not been able to decide to set his name to it. He knows from experience that books are often condemned from dislike for their author, and he also knows that an author's reputation gives a value to his work. Hence he remains in his present obscurity to secure a freer and juster verdict; nevertheless, he will make himself known if this story proves as agreeable to the public as he hopes."

la Fayette, and which the worthy gentleman afterward called his "Zaïde," — apparently from an excess of friendly zeal. It is, after all, very possible that he may have devised the plot of "Zaïde," and even that he may have written a few pages of the story. It is easy to imagine Segrais writing in the romantic style of this Spanish story; but it is impossible to see what he could have contributed to the "Princess of Clèves," the note of which is entirely different. Segrais' taste always inclined to grace and prettiness, — which certainly are not the characteristic qualities of the novel of 1678. We cannot even be certain that Segrais would in his heart have approved so simple a tale; he would have vastly preferred "Zaïde," his "Zaïde," with its abductions, its shipwrecks, its pirates, its gloomy solitudes, where flawless lovers breathed forth their sighs in palaces adorned with allegorical paintings. The "Princess of Clèves" appeared two years after the return of Segrais to Caen, the city of his birth.

The book was doubtless written before the academician left Madame de la Fayette's house; but even if he had assisted in its preparation, it was not his book, it was not his "Princess." As for the Duke of La Rochefoucauld, he was, as every one knows, the acknowledged lover of Madame de la Fayette; their relations were respected by every one, and many things combined to diminish the scandal of their intimacy. The duke was an old man; Madame de la Fayette was no longer young, and had never been beautiful; they were both ill, feeble, almost at the point of death. Lastly, he was a prince, and she was very devout. It was a natural supposition that they wrote their novels together, as Monsieur and Madame Dacier read Greek together. It was also known that the duke liked to read novels. He used to say, after having been loved by Madame de Sablé, by Madame de Longueville, and by Madame de la Fayette, that he had never known love outside of the pages of a novel. He was credited with a share in the "Princess of Clèves" only because it was possible that he might have had one; but no one knew how large this share was, or even whether there was one. For my part, I do not believe that he inspired or contributed a line. His imagination was powerful, but its flight was short; he grasped at everything, but everything slipped through his fingers. Moreover, he was weary of life;

while Madame de la Fayette, although she seemed almost at the last gasp, never eating or sleeping, parched with fever, withered, half dead, was yet very active and an indefatigable writer. Among other matters which she had undertaken, she had for twelve years been governing Savoy by letters, as the secret agent of the Regent. Huet testifies that he saw her write "Zaïde;" Madame de Sévigné, her most intimate friend, assigns to her, without a moment's hesitation, both the "Princess of Montpensier" and the "Princess of Clèves;" and I know no evidence that can be urged against this most probable statement except that of Madame de la Fayette herself.

The relations of Madame de la Fayette to the little court of Savoy were hidden in France from even the most intimate friends of that lady, and have eluded all her biographers. Sainte-Beuve himself, who seldom went astray, had no suspicion of the political intrigues which played a prominent part in a life which he supposed thoroughly filled with works of piety, with literature, and with an engrossing affection. It is not yet twelve years since Monsieur A. D. Perrero published the letters of Madame de la Fayette which he had discovered in the Turin archives.[1] These letters show us the sedate mistress of La Rochefoucauld in a new light,— busier, more interested in politics, in statesmanship, than might seem desirable. Doubtless she was working for France, and asked the most trivial

---

[1] Lettere inedite di Madame de Lafayette. Torino, 1880. See, too, the article by Arvède Barine in the "Revue des Deux Mondes" for Sept. 15, 1880.

rewards for her services; but it is a surprise to detect in her such an intriguing nature, and we must acknowledge that the excellent Madame de Sévigné, who called her so candid, did not know her at all. I should be unwilling to say that Madame de la Fayette was not candid, but it is very certain that she was extremely reserved and that she deceived every one. All who had anything to do with her imagined her continually lost in day-dreams; they called her misty: yet in reality she was most precise, most practical. Truthful she was, without doubt; yet there is one matter in which it is impossible to believe her, and that is when she denies having written the " Princess of Clèves."

This denial is to be found in a letter, written April 13, 1678, to the secretary of the Regent of Savoy Lescheraine, with whom the countess was carrying on a diplomatic correspondence. We quote the interesting part of this letter: —

"A little book which had some vogue fifteen years ago, and which the public was pleased to ascribe to me, has earned me the title of author of the 'Princess of Clèves.' But I assure you that I have had no part in it, and that Monsieur de la Rochefoucauld, who has also been mentioned, has had as little as I. He denies it so strenuously that it is impossible not to believe him, especially about a matter which can be confessed without shame. As for me, I am flattered at being suspected, and I think I should acknowledge the book if I was sure that the author would never claim it of me. I find it very agreeable, well-written, without being extremely polished, full of very delicate touches, and well worth more than a single reading; and what I especially notice is an exact representation of the persons composing the court and of their manner of life. It is without romanticism and exaggeration, and so is not a romance; it is more like a book of memoirs, — and I hear that was the first title of the book; but it was changed. There you have my opinion on the 'Princess of Clèves;' let me ask you for yours, for people have almost come to blows over it. Many blame what others praise; so, whatever you say, you will not find yourself alone in your views."

This letter makes it clear that Madame de la Fayette was averse to having it known, in Savoy at least, that she was a writer of books, and that she had been so called by Claude Barbin, the bookseller of the Palais. With one stroke of the pen she disclaims both the "Princess of Clèves" and "Zaïde," which had been published fifteen, or,

more accurately, seventeen years.¹ She
disavows any share in it, as does Monsieur de la Rochefoucauld, whose denial
she mentions. Yet she is far from condemning what she disclaims. She says
that if the "Princess of Clèves" is not
by her, she would be glad to have written it, and she is almost tempted to steal
it from its true author. She praises the
book more warmly than we should be
able to do. Save in sincerity, she reminds us of the poor girl who sighed
and said: "Children are so lovely! What
a pity that they bring disgrace!" Did
Madame de la Fayette look upon the
"Princess of Clèves" as a charming
sin, a sweet disgrace? I should be
inclined to think that she did. Later,
Voltaire was to give us many exam-

¹ We have said that "Zaïde" appeared in 1670. It was reprinted in 1705 and 1719.

ples of disavowals of this sort. But Voltaire lied with too much pleasure, with an unction that betrayed a natural predisposition to falsehood. This great enemy of prejudice never hesitated to employ a lie in the service of the truth. Sometimes he lied merely for his own pleasure, thereby swerving from the precept of a great master of the art, Monsieur de Talleyrand, who used to say: "Lying is such an excellent thing that it should not be abused." However that may be, it is easy to understand why Voltaire denied this or that one of his books. We are more surprised by Madame de la Fayette's disavowal, coming as it does from the most "candid" of women, and it is not easy to see what were her real reasons. Arvède Barine — in the article in the "Revue des Deux

Mondes" already cited — suggests that possibly Madame de la Fayette was afraid of offending the Regent of Savoy, a Princess of Nemours, by acknowledging herself to be the author of a novel in which a Nemours is represented as the handsomest man of his day, but as thoroughly devoted to gallantry.

This would be an excess of scrupulousness for which there was no occasion. The Regent, Marie de Nemours, commonly called Madame Royale, was also notorious for her many love affairs, which, indeed, she took no pains to conceal; and Monsieur de Nemours would no more have shocked her by his conduct than he would have displeased her by his appearance. Moreover, even if she had assumed a prudery which in no way belonged to her, no woman even of excessive religious sensitiveness would ever have blushed at having had a Nemours in her family.

I rather incline to think that Madame de la Fayette, who took pleasure in writing because she wrote well, was unwilling to be known as an author, especially at courts. It was she, we must say, who was prudish and pious. Now, about 1678 women writers enjoyed no very high repute. By her epoch and by her friendships Madame de la Fayette belonged to the brilliant society of the Fronde. Ever since she had been Mademoiselle de la Vergne, and showed Ménage how much more Latin she knew than he, the Hôtel de Rambouillet had set the fashion for a society very eager for fame, and no less critical in matters of feeling than in those of the intellect. At that time it was customary for women to combine pure morals with intellectual brilliancy. To be learned was to be virtuous; and wisdom in the ancient sense, as it was then understood, implied rhetoric, astronomy, and chastity. That is the way that Mademoiselle de la Vergne understood it, and she was very anxious to be thought learned. After her marriage, which brought her no happiness, she became intimate with the *précieuses*, who dealt in subtilties and affected to scorn the pleasures of the senses. Then it was that she brought out the "Princess of Montpensier;" but at that very moment public opinion was changing. The new generation showed itself severe toward those once famous women, and with some rudeness ordered them back to their domestic duties. The *précieuses* were ridiculed on all sides; they were attacked by Molière and by the Abbé de Pure at the same time. Madame de la Fayette, like a discreet woman, concealed her Latin and yielded to the new current of thought, although she felt that she had a genius for writing. While she risked "Zaïde" in the face of this reaction, when even Madeleine de Scudéry, that illustrious Sappho, passed for a tolerably ridiculous person, it was with the precautions we have mentioned, and behind the mask of Monsieur de Segrais. Eighteen years later, a woman as sensitive of her reputation as was Madame de la Fayette had still to be cautious about appearing in print. Women who wrote were looked upon as improper characters, and not wholly without reason. Madame Deshoulières had been loose in her life, Madame de la Suze still was, and Mademoiselle de Villedieu lived with an officer. Learned women like Madame de la Sablière made great concessions to the emotions. Madame de la Fayette was unwilling to seem learned, and entered the republic of letters only behind a triple veil. Besides, she was a woman of piety, and belonged to the little coterie of Port Royal, in which novels were an abomination. Monsieur Nicole, the gentlest of men, said at that time: " A writer of novels or plays is a public poisoner, not of men's bodies, but of the souls of the faithful; and he ought to look upon himself as guilty of numberless spiritual homicides, — whether, in fact, he has already caused them, or only may cause them by his pernicious writings." It is plain that Madame de la Fayette had, after all, some reasons for not too openly acknowledging the "Princess of Clèves."

The book which appeared in this mysterious way was at once successful. For a whole season every one was talking about it. Madame de la Fayette scarcely exaggerated when she spoke of people " coming to blows " about it. Young Valincour, the friend of Racine, wrote a criticism of it which was ascribed to Father Bouhours, and an Abbé de Charmes replied with an apology which appeared under the name of Barbier d'Aucour. Boursault made a tragedy out of it, for in France everything that acquires notoriety comes at last upon the stage.

Never was success better deserved. Madame de la Fayette was the first to introduce naturalness into fiction, — the first to draw human beings and real feelings; and thereby she earned a place among the true classics, — fitly following Molière, La Fontaine, Boileau, and Racine, who had brought back the Muses to nature and truth. "Andromaque" belongs to 1667; the "Princess of Clèves" to 1678: modern French literature starts from those two dates. The "Princess of Clèves" is the first French novel in which the interest depends on the truth of the passions.

But we must not forget that if this novel shows, by the charming simplicity of its style and thought, that Racine had appeared, introducing Monime and Bérénice, yet Madame de la Fayette, by the very spirit of her work, belongs to the generation of the Fronde and of Corneille. She remains heroic in her simplicity, and, like the author of "Cinna," preserves a proud and noble ideal of life. In the essential points of her character her heroine is, like Emilie, an "adorable fury," — a fury of modesty, it may be; but none the less a few serpents' heads appear to be concealed in her beautiful blond hair. The philosophy of Madame de la Fayette is like that of Corneille, and she held to the past as do women no longer young. Racine — and it was the great success of this genius, who was both charming and powerful — represented his tragic heroines as pathetic victims of their heart and of their senses. Corneille had exalted the will to a point of absurdity; Racine showed the omnipotence of the passions, and, without knowing it, he was in this respect the boldest of innovators. He introduced into poetry a new, unheard-of, profound truth. His contemporaries had no very clear vision of this; even those who, like Saint-Evremond, were to enter most readily into this philosophy, were restrained by their literary prejudices. Hence we need not be surprised that Madame de Sévigné felt a frivolous contempt for works so great that she was incompetent to understand them. Her intimate friend, Madame de la Fayette, was far more thoughtful and of keener intellect; she understood things whose existence the marchioness never even suspected. Nevertheless, in her study of the passions she clung, and insisted on clinging, to the psychology of Corneille and of the *précieuses*. What did she really think? No one will ever know. Her real personality was impenetrable; even her confessor did not know her. A prude, pious, with a high position at court, I can almost suspect her of having doubted of virtue, of having believed only faintly in God, and — what was more astonishing at that period — of having hated the king. I am convinced that she was a great freethinker. She never told her secret, not even in the "Princess of Clèves."

I shall not analyze this novel, which is familiar even to those who have not read it. It is well known that the scene is laid in the court of Henri II., but that in fact the manners described are those, somewhat idealized, of people of quality who lived at the same period as the author. Writers of the seventeenth century had no true sense of the past, and unconsciously delineated themselves under ancient or foreign names: thus Madame de la Fayette with perfect simplicity ascribes to the contemporaries of the Valois the lan-

guage and manners of the courtiers of
Louis XIV. I do not say that she was
not familiar with the epoch of the Valois,
I do say that she but dimly understood
it; and we should be glad that she did
not undertake to describe it, — that
would have been only a work of erudition, while, as it was, she gave free play
to her genius. It is scarcely worth while
to recall the simple story that is the
basis of this charming book. Madame
de Clèves, the most beautiful woman of
the court, is loved by Monsieur de Nemours, the most accomplished gentleman of the whole kingdom. Monsieur
de Nemours, though he had led a life
of gallantry, becomes timid as soon as
he is really in love. He hides his passion, but Madame de Clèves detects it,
and involuntarily shares it. To defend
herself from the danger to which her

heart exposes her, she finally decides to tell her husband that she loves Monsieur de Nemours, that she fears him and fears herself. Her husband at first reassures and consoles her; but through the imprudence and an indiscretion of the Duke of Nemours he imagines himself wronged, and dies of grief. His widow does not judge that she has thereby regained her liberty; she remains faithful to the memory of a husband whom she had never loved.

That in many ways seems admirable. It is true that Madame de Clèves sets a high value on virtue, for she does not think it is paid too high a price by the death of the husband and the despair of a lover, — taking this last word in the sense that it had in the seventeenth century. "What do you think of it?" I asked a woman whose honest and intelligent mind I admire. This was what she was good enough to reply: —

"Except for her preciosity, the Princess of Clèves is a true heroine of the Hôtel de Rambouillet. She is divine like Clélie and Arthénice. Her beauty is unrivalled, her soul knows no weakness. But Madame de Clèves is no artificial heroine, and the motives that inspire her have their roots in reality, and do not depend on fiction. Her principles are very human, and wholly without any ideal; propriety and reason, which are transient virtues, control her life and regulate her feelings. And even more than propriety, the notion of her worldly position fills and protects her. She has the profoundest respect for appearances, and her aristocratic pride mitigates many of her secret sufferings. I fancy that to this woman, whose psychology, and especially whose moral nature, was so much less complicated than ours, the world must have seemed like a well-lighted drawing-room, and that her duty consisted in passing through it with dignity and grace; then with a majestic courtesy she withdrew, and all was over. It is the triumph of etiquette, and of etiquette which may amount to heroism; for it sometimes takes more courage and more firmness to smile in the midst of a ball than on the battle-field. The Princess of Clèves possesses that sort of courage, — she possesses it to such an extent that she forgets herself and sacrifices herself; she has no weakness, but she also has no pity. She gives over to despair and death two men, one of whom at least she loves. She has no remorse, because she has given no cause for scandal, and nothing has seriously marred the happy harmony of her conduct. She is an excellent example of what is produced by very rigid social principles and a very severe rule of life with nothing higher than these principles. She is also an edifying, though discouraging, instance of what morality and virtue can do for men's happiness. In contrast with this loyal and unflinching soul, we recall those other heroines who were weak, who were guilty, but were gentle; and we ask if, underlying lofty virtue, there was not a feeling of pride which consoled her for everything, even for the harm she wrought."

Doubtless what is most original in the conduct of Madame de Clèves is her confession to her husband of her love for another man. This cannot be regarded as a kind action, for this confession is the primary cause of the death of Monsieur de Clèves. If she had not spoken, Monsieur de Clèves would not have died; he would have lived on, tranquilly, happily, in an agreeable delusion: but truth was required at all hazards. This was also the opinion of a famous woman who a hundred years later repeated this confession. Madame Roland, when thirty-nine years old, felt "the strong affections of a powerful mind controlling a robust body." The man she loved had, like her, a lofty feeling of duty. He was the Deputy Buzot. They loved, but that was all. Madame Roland had a husband twenty years older than she, and decrepit. She thought it her duty, following the example of Madame de Clèves, to confess to him that she loved another man; but the confession once made, this half-dead husband could not take it tragically, so that perhaps in this respect Madame Roland will seem less imprudent than Madame de Clèves. In spite of that, she had no reason to be satisfied with her confession of the state of affairs to him, as she acknowledges in her Memoirs: —

"I honor and cherish my husband as an affectionate daughter adores a virtuous father for whom she would sacrifice even a lover;

but I have found the man who might be this lover, and while I remained faithful to my duties my ingenuity has not been able to hide the feelings that I sacrificed to them. My husband, whose susceptibility and self-love were both easily roused, could not endure the idea of the slightest modification in sway; he imagined dark things; his jealousy annoyed me; happiness fled far from us. He adored me; I sacrificed myself to him, and we were wretched. Were I free, I would follow him anywhere, to soothe his sufferings and to console his old age: a soul like mine is contented with no imperfect sacrifice. But Roland detests the thought of a sacrifice; and having once perceived that I am making one for him, the knowledge destroys all his happiness. It pains him to receive such a sacrifice, and yet he cannot do without it."

Roland did not die of this. Every one says that he was sublime; and he promised some time to make way for the man who was loved, if his wife's new affection should continue. Madame Roland was also sublime, and refused to hear of this generous sacrifice. But sublime as they were, they quarrelled and grew more bitter. The household was most unhappy when the 31st of May brought them other cares, and swept away their domestic bickerings in the public disaster.

So far as I know, the cruel frankness of Madame de Clèves has been imitated by no other woman than Madame Roland. I do not dare to say that this is to be regretted; but however it may be, we must in justice remember that for acting as she did, Madame Roland had not such good reasons as Madame de Clèves. Madame de Clèves when she confided in her husband asked for his aid in

her distress, she implored his support;
Madame Roland merely wanted to expose her passion, — and those are two
very different things. As for Madame
de la Fayette, she was so delighted
with these tragic confessions that she
afterward wrote a novel simply to show
another woman making the same confession under still more painful circumstances; for she is guilty, and confesses
to her husband that she has deceived
him. The Countess of Tende, who
takes her husband for the confidant of
her weaknesses, outdoes even Madame
Roland in heroic sincerity.

She is another candid woman. It
is amusing that these candid women
should have sprung from the imagination of a woman who never confessed
even to her confessor.

ANATOLE FRANCE.

P. S. I thought that I had kept within bounds, that I had justly admired the "Princess of Clèves" and justly esteemed Madame de la Fayette; but justice is not everything. To a masterpiece, to a woman, something besides justice is due, and I became uneasy. I feared that I had been deficient in that politeness, that courtesy, without which even the belles-lettres remain rude and unpolished. Hence, remembering that Auguste Comte had admitted the "Princess of Clèves" into the Positivist Library, I took the liberty of asking the heir of the founder, the venerable leader of the Positivists, to be good enough to write for me a few words about this princess, which he admires, as I know, with an intelligent fervor. Monsieur Pierre Laffitte was kind enough to reply; and here is his letter, which will correct my preface. This letter is just what I expected from a philosopher animated, like the ancient Epicurus, by an ardent enthusiasm for reason.

Paris, December 28, 1888.
[28 Bichat, 100 Gall.]

My dear Monsieur France, — I am glad to see that you have written about the "Princess of Clèves," and I am sure that you will not take amiss a few observations, not on its literary qualities, for there would be but little propriety in my addressing you on this score, but merely on the state of mind which this masterpiece indicates, — all the more that it does this without premeditation.

What has always struck me in reading this distinguished product of the female mind is the complete absence of everything supernatural. The name of God is not once mentioned; and yet the inner working of human life, and more especially of a woman's life, is portrayed without any appearance of strangeness or want of logic; and that is so true that no one before me, so far as I know, has ever noticed this absence of God. Read more particularly that wonderful discussion in which Madame de Clèves sets forth her reasons for refusing to marry Monsieur de Nemours. The reasons influencing her in forming this most important decision are all of a perfectly natural sort; she succeeds in overcoming a deep and lawful attachment by delicate and wise motives. The absence of the supernatural is all the more striking here, from the fact that human motives assure the superiority of reason over the passions, and not their mere brutal victory.

It is evident that a work of this sort portrays a new state of mental equilibrium attained by a woman, — it is true, by a very superior woman, — in whom life is controlled by the appreciation of the consequences of our actions, without thought of any supernatural interference. Women of a rare type have reached this lofty state, in which life has become wise, dignified, and delicate, void of fear as well as of what, for the sake of politeness, I will not call a chimerical, but at least a doubtful, hope. For this is not peculiar to Madame de la Fayette; read Madame de Lambert's "Advice to my Son," and you will see that, with the exception of a few formulas of politeness toward God, every motive for living with dignity is of a human sort. Is not this a practical demonstration of the possibility of conceiving of a life, not only honorable but lofty and delicate, by considerations of a merely natural order? The demonstration is all the more striking because it is in no way systematic, — no attempt is made to prove anything; it is merely described. The slow evolution of humanity has produced such a condition in superior souls, — which, after all, are only in advance of the rest; the systematization will follow later.

Doubtless I shall be told that the supernatural scaffolding was necessary at first, — I grant it; but they at least have succeeded in doing without it. Thus man does not really belong to the animal kingdom. This becomes serious in large societies; consequently, the leaders of our race sought at first to provide against it. But they had to invoke both a God and a Devil to persuade men to act nobly. At the present time the West gets along without fear of hell or hope of paradise. Why may not the evolution accomplished by civilized peoples in a simple case be also attained in more complicated cases? The "Princess of Clèves" furnishes us with the demonstration, not by scholastic rules, but by a living figure, in an æsthetic masterpiece; and this absence of God helps to portray the final victory of reason over passion, which is the normal type of our species.

But let us consider the opposite opinion, and by discussing art, not science. Jean-Jacques Rousseau, in a period of reaction, introduced God again; read the "Nouvelle Héloïse," and see what a part he makes him play there: it must be said, with all possible politeness, that it is a sorry one. God intervenes to justify tender weaknesses, or at least to accept them with a smiling tolerance. And in the nineteenth century how this tendency has developed! In George Sand, when women wish to yield gracefully, God is always there to make things easy for them. He has to play a singular part. We are very far from those momentous decisions in which the soul exercises control, such as Madame de la Fayette described with a thorough knowledge of human nature.

On the whole, the "Princess of Clèves" seems to me the most perfect work that ever issued from a woman's hand. She did not try works of vast strength in any direction, but in her own field Madame de la Fayette had complete mastery.

Preface.

Her book will be read so long as there shall survive men of taste and intelligence; it is a pleasure to feel one's self in communion with the chosen spirits who, since the seventeenth century, have enjoyed this delightful masterpiece, and to think of the others who, after us, will still enjoy it.

P. LAFFITTE.

THE PRINCESS OF CLÈVES.

PART I.

THERE never was in France so brilliant a display of magnificence and gallantry as during the last years of the reign of Henri II. This monarch was gallant, handsome, and susceptible; although his love for Diane de Poitiers, Duchess of Valentinois, had lasted twenty years, its ardor had not diminished, as his conduct testified.

He was remarkably skilful in physical exercises, and devoted much attention to them; every day was filled with hunting and tennis, dancing, running at the ring, and sports of that kind. The favorite colors and the initials of Madame de Valentinois were to be seen everywhere, and she herself used to appear dressed as richly as Mademoiselle de la Marck, her granddaughter, who was then about to be married.

The fact that the queen was there, accounted for her presence. This princess, although she had passed her first youth, was still beautiful; she was fond of splendor, magnificence, and pleasure. The king had married her while still Duke of Orléans, in the lifetime of his elder brother, the dauphin, who afterward died at Tournon, mourned as a worthy heir to the position of Francis I., his father.

The queen's ambition made her like to reign. She seemed indifferent to the king's attachment to the Duchess of Valentinois, and never betrayed any jealousy; but she was so skilled a dissembler that it was hard to discover her real feelings, and she was compelled by policy to keep the duchess near her if she wanted to see anything of the king. As for him, he liked the society of women, even of those with whom he was not at all in love. He was with the queen every day at her audience, when all the most attractive lords and ladies were sure to appear.

At no court had there ever been gathered together so many lovely women and brave men. It seemed as if Nature had made an effort to show her highest beauty in the greatest lords and ladies. Madame Elisabeth of France, afterwards queen of Spain, began to show her wonderful intelligence and that unrivalled beauty which was so fatal to her. Mary Stuart, the queen of Scotland, who had just married the dauphin and was called the crown princess, or dauphiness, was faultless in mind and body. She had been brought up at the French court and had acquired all its polish; she was endowed by Nature with so strong a love for the softer graces that in spite of her youth she admired and understood them perfectly. Her mother-in-law, the queen, and Madame, the king's sister, were also fond of poetry, of comedy, and of music. The interest which King Francis I. had felt in poetry and letters still prevailed in France, and since the king, his son, was devoted to physical exercise, pleasures of all sorts were to be found at the court. But what rendered the court especially fine and majestic was the great number of princes and lords of exceptional merit; those I am about to name were, in their different ways, the ornament and the admiration of their age.

The King of Navarre inspired universal respect by his exalted rank and his royal bearing. He excelled in the art of war; but the Duke of Guise had shown himself so strong a rival that he had often laid aside his command to enter the duke's service as a private soldier in the most dangerous battles. This duke had manifested such admirable bravery with such remarkable success that he was an object of envy to every great commander. He had many conspicuous qualities besides his personal courage, — he possessed a vast and profound intelligence, a noble, lofty mind, and equal capacity for war and affairs. His brother, the Cardinal of Lorraine, was born with an unbridled ambition, and had acquired vast learning; this he turned to his profit by using it in defence of Catholicism, which had begun to be attacked. The Chevalier de Guise, afterwards known as the Grand Prior, was loved by all; he was handsome, witty, clever, and his courage was renowned throughout Europe. The short, ill-favored body of the Prince of Condé held a great and haughty soul, and an intelligence that endeared him to even the most beautiful women. The Duke of Nevers, famous for his military prowess and his important services to the state, though somewhat advanced in years was adored by all the court. He had three handsome sons, — the second, known as the Prince of Clèves, was worthy to bear that proud title; he was brave and grand, and was withal endowed with a prudence rare in the young. The Vidame of Chartres, a scion of the old house of Vendôme, a name not despised by princes of the blood, had won equal triumphs in war and gallantry; he was handsome, attractive, brave, hardy, generous; all his good qualities were distinct and striking, — in short, he was the only man fit to be compared, if such comparison be possible, with the Duke of Nemours. This nobleman was a masterpiece of Nature; the least of his fascinations was his extreme beauty; he was the handsomest man in the world. What made him superior to every one else was his unrivalled courage and a charm manifested in his mind, his expression, and his actions, such as no other showed. He possessed a certain playfulness that was equally attractive to men and women; he was unusually skilful in physical exercises; and he dressed in a way that every one tried in vain to imitate; moreover, his bearing was such that all eyes followed him wherever he appeared.

There was no lady in the court who would not have been flattered by his attentions; few of those to whom he had devoted himself could boast of having resisted him; and even many in whom he had shown no interest made very clear their affection for him. He was so gentle and courteous that he could not refuse some attentions to those who tried to please him, — hence he had many mistresses; but it was hard to say whom he really loved. He was often to be seen with the dauphiness; her beauty, her gentleness, her desire to please every one, and the especial regard she showed for this prince, made some imagine that he dared to raise his eyes to her. The Guises, whose niece she was, had acquired influence and position by her marriage; they aspired to an equality with the princes of the blood and to a share of the power exercised by the Constable of Montmorency. It was to the constable that the king confided the greater part of the cares of state, while he treated the Duke of Guise and the Marshal of Saint-André as his favorites. But those attached to his person by favor or position could only keep their place by submitting to the Duchess of Valentinois, who, although no longer young or beautiful, ruled him so despotically that she may be said to have been the mistress of his person and of the state.

The king had always loved the constable, and at the beginning of his reign had summoned him from the exile into which he had been sent by Francis I. The court was divided between the Guises and the constable, who was the favorite of the princes of the blood. Both parties had always struggled for the favor of the Duchess of Valentinois. The Duke of Aumale, brother of the Duke of Guise, had married one of her daughters. The constable aspired to the same alliance, not satisfied with having married his eldest son to Madame Diane, a daughter of the king by a lady of Piedmont who entered a convent after the birth of her child. The promises which Monsieur de Montmorency had made to Mademoiselle de Piennes, one of the queen's maids-of-honor, had proved a serious obstacle to this match; and although the king had removed it with extreme patience and kindness, the constable still felt insecure until he had won over the Duchess of Valentinois and had separated her from the Guises, whose greatness had begun to alarm her. She had delayed in every way in her power the marriage between the dauphin and the Queen of Scotland; this young queen's beauty and intelligence, and the position given to the Guises by this marriage, were very odious to her. She especially detested the Cardinal of Lorraine, who had addressed her in bitter, even contemptuous terms. She saw that he was intriguing with the queen; hence the constable found her ready to join forces with him by bringing about the marriage of Mademoiselle de la Marck, her granddaughter, to Monsieur d'Anville, his second son, who succeeded to his post in the reign of Charles IX. The constable did not expect that Monsieur d'Anville would have any objections to this marriage, as had been the case with Monsieur de Montmorency; but though the reasons were more hidden, the difficulties were no less obstinate. Monsieur d'Anville was desperately in love with the crown princess; and although his passion was hopeless, he could not persuade himself to contract other ties. The Marshal of Saint-André was almost the only courtier who had taken sides with neither faction; he was one of the favorites, but this position he held simply by his own merits. Ever since he had been the dauphin, the king had been attached to this nobleman, and later had made him marshal of France, at an age when men are satisfied with lesser honors. His advance gave him a distinction which he maintained by his personal worth and charm, by a costly table and rich surroundings, and by more splendor than any private individual had yet displayed. The king's generosity warranted this sumptuousness. There was no limit to this monarch's generosity to those he loved. He did not possess every great quality, but he had many, and among them the love of war and a good knowledge of it. This accounted for his many successes; and if we except the battle of St. Quentin, his reign was an unbroken series of victories. He had won the battle of Renty in person, Piedmont had been conquered, the English had been driven from France, and the Emperor Charles V. had seen his good fortune desert him before the city of Metz, which he had besieged in vain with all the forces of the Empire and of Spain. Nevertheless, since the defeat of St. Quentin had diminished our hope of conquest, and fortune seemed to favor one king as much as the other, they were gradually led to favor peace.

The Dowager Duchess of Lorraine had begun to lead the way to a cessation of hostilities at the time of the dauphin's marriage, and ever since then there had been secret negotiations. At last Cercamp, in the Province of Artois, was chosen as the place of meeting. The Cardinal of Lorraine, the constable, and the Marshal of Saint-André appeared in behalf of the King of France; the Duke of Alva and the Prince of Orange in behalf of Philip II. The Duke and Duchess of Lorraine were the mediators. The leading articles were the marriage of Madame Elisabeth of France to Don Carlos, Infanta of Spain, and that of Madame, the king's sister, with Monsieur de Savoie.

Meanwhile the king remained on the frontier, and there heard of the death of Mary, queen of England. He sent the Count of Randan to Elizabeth to congratulate her on ascending the throne. She was very glad to receive him, because her rights were so insecure that it was of great service to her to have them acknowledged by the king. The count found her well informed about the interests of France and the capabilities of those who composed the court, but especially familiar with the reputation of the Duke of Nemours. She spoke of this nobleman so often and with such warmth that when Monsieur de Randan returned and recounted his journey to the king, he told him that there was nothing to which Monsieur de Nemours could not aspire, and that she would be capable of marrying him. That very evening the king spoke to this nobleman, and made Monsieur de Randan repeat to him his conversation with Elizabeth, urging him to essay this great fortune. At first Monsieur de Nemours thought that the king was jesting; but when he saw his mistake he said, —

"At any rate, sire, if I undertake a fantastic enterprise under the advice and in behalf of your Majesty, I beg of you to keep it secret until success shall justify me before the public, and to guard me from appearing vain enough to suppose that a queen who has never seen me should wish to marry me from love."

The king promised to speak of the plan to no one but the constable, and agreed that secrecy was essential for its success. Monsieur de Randan advised Monsieur de Nemours to visit England as a simple traveller; but the latter could not make up his mind to do this. He sent Lignerolles, an intelligent young man, one of his favorites, to ascertain the queen's feeling and to try to open the matter. Meanwhile he went to see the Duke of Savoy, who was then at Brussels with the King of Spain. The death of Mary of England raised great obstacles to any treaty of peace; the commission broke up at the end of November, and the king returned to Paris.

At that moment there appeared at court a young lady to whom all eyes were turned, and we may well believe that she was possessed of faultless beauty, since she aroused admiration where all were well accustomed to the sight of handsome women. Of the same family as the Vidame of Chartres, she was one of the greatest heiresses in France. Her father had died young, leaving her under the charge of his wife, Madame de Chartres, whose kindness, virtue, and worth were beyond praise. After her husband's death she had withdrawn from court for many years; during this period she had devoted herself to the education of her daughter, not merely cultivating her mind and her beauty, but also seeking to inspire her with the love of virtue and to make her attractive. Most mothers imagine that it is enough never to speak of gallantry to their daughters to guard them from it forever. Madame de Chartres was of a very different opinion; she often drew pictures of love to her daughter, showing her its fascinations, in order to give her a better understanding of its perils. She told her how insincere men are, how false and deceitful; she described the domestic miseries which illicit love-affairs entail, and, on the other hand, pictured to her the peaceful happiness of a virtuous woman's life, as well as the distinction and elevation which virtue gives to a woman of rank and beauty. She taught her, too, how hard it was to preserve this virtue without extreme care, and without that one sure means of securing a wife's happiness, which is to love her husband and to be loved by him.

This heiress was, then, one of the greatest matches in France, and although she was very young, many propositions of marriage had been made to her. Madame de Chartres, who was extremely proud, found almost nothing worthy of her daughter, and the girl being in her sixteenth year, she was anxious to take her to court. The Vidame went to welcome her on her arrival, and was much struck by the marvellous beauty of Mademoiselle de Chartres, — and with good reason : her delicate complexion and her blond hair gave her a unique brilliancy; her features were regular, and her face and person were full of grace and charm.

The day after her arrival she went to match some precious stones at the house of an Italian who dealt in them. He had come from Florence with the queen, and had grown so rich by his business that his house seemed that of some great nobleman rather than of a merchant. The Prince of Clèves happened to come in while she was there; he was so struck by her beauty that he could not conceal his surprise, and Mademoiselle de Chartres could not keep from blushing when she saw his astonishment: she succeeded, however, in regaining her composure without paying any further attention to the prince than civility required for a man of his evident importance. Monsieur de Clèves gazed at her admiringly, wondering who this beauty was whom he did not know. He perceived from her bearing and her suite that she must be a lady of high rank. She was so young that he thought she must be unmarried; but since she had not her mother with her, and the Italian, who did not know her, addressed her as "madame," he was in great doubt, and stared at her with continual surprise. He saw that his glances embarrassed her, unlike most young women, who always take pleasure in seeing the effect of their beauty; it even seemed to him that his presence made her anxious to go away, and in fact she left very soon. Monsieur de Clèves consoled himself for her departure with the hope of finding out who she was, and was much disappointed to learn that no one knew. He was so struck by her beauty and evident modesty that from that moment he conceived for her the greatest love and esteem. That evening he called on Madame, the king's sister.

This princess was held in high esteem on account of her influence with the king, her brother; and this influence was so great that when the king made peace he consented to restore Piedmont to enable her to marry

J. Garnier inv.   A. Lamotte sc.

Monsieur de Savoie. Although she had always meant to marry, she had determined to give her hand to none but a sovereign, and had for that reason refused the King of Navarre when he was Duke of Vendôme, and had always felt an interest in Monsieur de Savoie after seeing him at Nice on the occasion of the interview between Francis I. and Pope Paul III. Since she possessed great intelligence and a fine taste, she drew pleasant persons about her, and at certain hours the whole court used to visit her.

Thither Monsieur de Clèves went, as was his habit. He was so full of the wit and beauty of Mademoiselle de Chartres that he could speak of nothing else; he talked freely of his adventure, and set no limit to his praise of the young woman he had seen but did not know. Madame said to him that there was no such person as he described, and that if there were, every one would have known about her. Madame de Dampierre, her lady-in-waiting and a friend of Madame de Chartres, when she heard the conversation moved near the princess and said to her in a low voice that doubtless it was Mademoiselle de Chartres whom Monsieur de Clèves had seen. Madame turned towards him and said that if he would return the next day, she would show him this beauty who had so impressed him. Mademoiselle de Chartres made her appearance the next day. The queen received her with every imaginable attention, and she was greeted with such admiration by every one that she heard around her nothing but praise. This she received with such noble modesty that she seemed not to hear it, or at least not to be affected by it. Then she visited the apartments of Madame, the king's sister. The princess, after praising her beauty, told her the surprise she had given to Monsieur de Clèves. A moment after, that person appeared.

"Come," she said to him, "see if I have not kept my word, and if, when I point out Mademoiselle de Chartres to you, I do not show you the beauty you sought; at any rate, thank me for telling her how much you already admire her."

Monsieur de Clèves was filled with joy to find that this young woman whom he had found so attractive was of a rank proportionate to her beauty. He went up to her and asked her to remember that he had been the first to admire her, and that without knowing her he had felt all the respect and esteem that were her due.

The Chevalier de Guise, his friend, and he left the house together. At first they praised Mademoiselle de Chartres without stint; then they found that they were praising her too much, and both stopped saying what they thought of her: but they were compelled to talk about her on the following days wherever they met. This new beauty was for a long time the general subject of conversation. The queen praised her warmly and showed an extraordinary regard for her; the dauphiness made her one of her favorites, and begged Madame de Chartres to bring her to see her very often; the daughters of the king invited her to all their entertainments, — in short, she was loved and admired by the whole court, except by Madame de Valentinois. It was not that this new beauty gave her any uneasiness, — her long experience had made her sure of the king, — but she so hated the Vidame of Chartres, whom she had desired to ally with herself by the marriage of one of her daughters, while he had joined the queen's party, that she could not look with favor on any one who bore his name and seemed to enjoy his friendship.

The Prince of Clèves fell passionately in love with Mademoiselle de Chartres, and was eager to marry her; but he feared lest the pride of Madame de Chartres should prevent her from giving her daughter to a man who was not the eldest of his family. Yet this family was so distinguished, and the Count of Eu, who was the head of the house, had just married a woman so near to royalty, that it was timidity rather than any true reason that inspired the fear of Monsieur de Clèves. He had many rivals; the Chevalier de Guise seemed to him the most formidable, on account of his birth, his ability, and the brilliant position of his family. This prince had fallen in love with Mademoiselle de Chartres the first day he saw her; he had noticed the passion of Monsieur de Clèves just as the latter had noticed his. Though the two men were friends, the separation which resulted from this rivalry gave them no chance to explain themselves, and their friendship cooled without their having courage to come to an understanding. The good fortune of Monsieur de Clèves in being the first to see Mademoiselle de Chartres seemed to him a happy omen, and to promise him some advantage over his rivals; but he foresaw serious obstacles on the part of the Duke of Nevers, his father. This duke was bound to the Duchess of Valentinois by many ties; she was an

enemy of the Vidame, and this was reason
enough to prevent the Duke of Nevers from
consenting that his son should think of that
nobleman's niece.

Madame de Chartres, who had already
taken such pains to fill her daughter with a
love of virtue, did not remit them in this
place where they were still so necessary, and
bad examples were so frequent. Ambition and gallantry were the sole occupation
of the court, busying men and women alike.
There were so many interests and so many
different intrigues in which women took part
that love was always mingled with politics,
and politics with love. No one was calm
or indifferent; every one sought to rise, to
please, to serve, or to injure; no one was
weary or idle, every one was taken up with
pleasure or intrigue. The ladies had their
special interest in the queen, in the crown
princess, in the Queen of Navarre, in Madame
the king's sister, or in the Duchess of Valentinois, according to their inclinations, their

sense of right, or their humor. Those who had passed their first youth and assumed an austere virtue, were devoted to the queen; those who were younger and sought pleasure and gallantry, paid their court to the crown princess. The Queen of Navarre had her favorites; she was young, and had much influence over her husband the king, who was allied with the constable, and hence highly esteemed. Madame the king's sister still preserved some of her beauty, and gathered several ladies about herself. The Duchess of Valentinois was sought by all those whom she deigned to regard; but the women she liked were few, and with the exception of those who enjoyed her intimacy and confidence, and whose disposition bore some likeness to her own, she received only on the days when she assumed to hold a court like the queen.

All these different cliques were separated by rivalry and envy. Then, too, the women who belonged to each one of them were also jealous of one another, either about their chances of advancement, or about their lovers; often their interests were complicated by other pettier, but no less important questions. Hence there was in this court a sort of well-ordered agitation, which rendered it very charming, but also very dangerous, for a young woman. Madame de Chartres saw this peril, and thought only of protecting her daughter from it. She besought her, not as a mother, but as a friend, to confide to her all the sweet speeches that might be made to her, and promised her aid in all those matters which so often embarrass the young.

The Chevalier de Guise made his feelings for Mademoiselle de Chartres and his intentions so manifest that every one could see them; yet he well knew the very grave difficulties that stood in his way. He was aware that he was not a desirable match, because his fortune was too small for his rank. He knew, too, that his brothers would disapprove of his marrying, through fear of the loss of position which sometimes befalls great families through the marriage of younger sons. The Cardinal of Lorraine soon proved to him that his fears were well grounded, for he denounced the chevalier's love for Mademoiselle de Chartres very warmly, though he concealed his true reasons. The cardinal nourished a hatred for the Vidame, which was hidden at the time, and only broke out later. He would have preferred to see his brother ally himself with any other family than that of the Vidame, and gave such public expression to his dislike that Madame de Chartres was plainly offended. She took great pains to show that the Cardinal of Lorraine had no cause for fear, and that she herself never contemplated the match. The Vidame adopted the same course, and with a better understanding of the cardinal's objection, because he knew the underlying reason.

The Prince of Clèves had concealed his passion quite as little as had the Chevalier de

Guise. The Duke of Nevers was sorry to hear of this attachment, but thought that his son would forget it at a word from him; great was his surprise when he found him determined to marry Mademoiselle de Chartres. He opposed this determination with a warmth so ill concealed that the whole court soon had wind of it, and it came to the knowledge of her mother. She had never doubted that Monsieur de Nevers would regard this match as an advantageous one for his son, and was much surprised that both the house of Clèves and that of Guise dreaded the alliance instead of desiring it. She was so chagrined that she sought to marry her daughter to some one who could raise her above those who fancied themselves superior to her; and after carefully going over the ground, pitched on the prince dauphin, the son of the Duke of Montpensier. He was of the right age to marry, and held the highest position at court. Since Madame de Chartres was a very clever woman, and was aided by the Vidame, who at that time had great influence, while her daughter was in every way a good match, she played her cards so cleverly and successfully that Monsieur de Montpensier appeared to desire the marriage, and it seemed as if nothing could stand in its way.

The Vidame, though aware of Monsieur d'Anville's devotion to the crown princess, still thought that he might make use of the influence which she had over him to induce him to speak well of Mademoiselle de Chartres to the king and to the Prince of Montpensier, whose intimate friend he was. He mentioned this to the princess, who took up the matter eagerly, since it promised advancement to a young woman of whom she had become very fond. This she told the Vidame, assuring him that though she knew she should offend her uncle, the Cardinal of Lorraine, this would be no objection, because she had good grounds for disliking him, since he every day furthered the queen's interests in opposition to her own.

Persons in love are always glad of any excuse for talking about the object of their affection. As soon as the Vidame had gone, the crown princess ordered Châtelart, the favorite of Monsieur d'Anville and the confidant of his love for her, to tell him to be at the queen's reception that evening. Châtelart received this command with great delight. He belonged to a good family of Dauphiné, but his merit and intelligence had raised him to a higher place than his birth warranted. He was received and treated with kindness by all the great lords at the court, and the favor of the family of Montmorency had attached him especially to Monsieur d'Anville. He was handsome and skilled in all physical exercises; he sang agreeably, wrote verses, and had a gallant, ardent nature, which so attracted Monsieur d'Anville that he made him a confidant of his love for the crown princess. The confidence brought him into the society of that lady, and thus began that unhappy passion, which robbed him of his reason and finally cost him his life.

Monsieur d'Anville did not fail to make his appearance that evening in the queen's drawing-room; he was pleased that the dauphiness had chosen him to aid her, and he promised faithfully to obey her commands. But Madame de Valentinois had heard of the contemplated marriage and had laid her plans to thwart it; she had been so successful in arousing the king's opposition that when Monsieur d'Anville spoke of it, he showed his disapproval, and commanded him to apprise the Prince of Montpensier of it. It is easy to imagine the feelings of Madame de Chartres at the failure of a plan she had so much desired, especially when her ill-success gave so great an advantage to her enemies and did so much harm to her daughter.

The crown princess kindly expressed to Mademoiselle de Chartres her regrets at not being able to further her interests. "You see," she said, "I have but very little power; I am so detested by the queen and the Duchess of Valentinois that they or their attendants always oppose everything I desire. Still," she added, "I have always tried to please them, and they hate me only on account of my mother, who used to fill them with uneasiness and jealousy. The king had been in love with her before he loved Madame de Valentinois, and in his early married life, before he had any children, though he loved this duchess, he seemed bent on dissolving that marriage to marry the queen my mother. Madame de Valentinois dreaded the woman he had loved so well, lest her wit and beauty should diminish her own power, and entered into an alliance with the constable, who was also opposed to the king's marrying a sister of the Guises. They won over the late king; and though he hated the Duchess of Valentinois as much as he loved the queen, he joined with them in preventing the king from dissolving his marriage. In order to make this impossible, they arranged my mother's marriage with the King of Scotland, whose first wife had been Madame Magdeleine, the king's sister, — this they did because it was the first thing that offered; though they broke the promises that had been made to the King of England, who was deeply in love with her. In fact, this matter nearly caused a falling out between the two kings. Henry VIII. could not be consoled for not marrying my mother; and whenever any other French princess was proposed to him, he used to say that she would never take the place of the one they had taken from him. It is true that my mother was a perfect beauty, and it is remarkable that when she was the widow of a duke of Longueville, three kings should have wanted to marry her. It was her misfortune to be married to the least important of them all, and to be sent to a kingdom where she has found nothing but unhappiness. I am told that I am like her; I dread the same sad fate, and whatever happiness seems to be awaiting me, I doubt if I ever enjoy it."

Mademoiselle de Chartres assured the crown princess that these gloomy presentiments were so fantastic that they could not long disturb her, and that she ought not to doubt that her good fortune would give the lie to her fears.

Henceforth no one dared to think of Mademoiselle de Chartres, through fear of displeasing the king or of not succeeding in winning a young woman who had aspired to a prince of the blood. None of these considerations moved Monsieur de Clèves. The death of his father, the Duke of Nevers, which happened at that time, left him free to follow his own inclinations, and as soon as the period of mourning had passed, he thought of nothing but marrying Mademoiselle de Chartres. He was glad to make his proposal at a time when circumstances had driven away all rivals and when he felt almost sure that she would not refuse him. What dimmed his joy was the fear of not being agreeable to her; and he would have preferred the happiness of pleasing her to the certainty of marrying her when she did not love him.

The Chevalier de Guise had somewhat aroused his jealousy; but since this was inspired more by his rival's merits than by the conduct of Mademoiselle de Chartres, he thought of nothing but ascertaining whether by good fortune she would approve of his designs. He met her only at the queen's rooms or in company, yet he managed to speak to her of his intentions and hopes in the most respectful way; he begged her to let him know how she felt towards him, and told her that his feelings for her were such that he should be forever unhappy if she obeyed her mother only from a sense of duty.

Mademoiselle de Chartres, having a very noble heart, was really grateful to the Prince of Clèves for what he did. This gratitude lent to her answer a certain gentleness, which was quite sufficient to feed the hope of a man as much in love as he was, and he counted on attaining at least a part of what he desired.

Mademoiselle repeated this conversation to her mother, who said that Monsieur de Clèves was of such high birth, possessed so many fine qualities, and seemed so discreet for a man of his age, that if she inclined to marry him she would herself gladly give her consent. Mademoiselle de Chartres replied that she had noticed the same fine qualities, and that she would rather marry him than any one else, but that she had no special love for him.

The next day the prince had his offer formally made to Madame de Chartres; she accepted it, being willing to give her daughter a husband she did not love. The marriage settlement was drawn up, the king was told of it, and the marriage became known to every one.

Monsieur de Clèves was very happy, although not perfectly satisfied; it gave him much pain to see that what Mademoiselle de Chartres felt for him was only esteem and gratitude, and he could not flatter himself that she nourished any warmer feeling; for had she done so, she would have readily shown it in their closer intimacy. Within a few days he complained to her of this.

"Is it possible," he said, "that I may not be happy in my marriage? Yet assuredly I am not happy. You have a sort of kindly feeling for me which cannot satisfy me; you are not impatient, uneasy, or grieved: you are as indifferent to my love as if this were given to your purse, and not to your charms."

"You do wrong to complain," she replied. "I do not know what more you can ask; it seems to me that you have no right to demand anything more."

"It is true," he said, "that you have a certain air with which I should be satisfied if there were anything behind it; but instead of your being restrained by a sense of propriety, it is a sense of propriety which inspires your actions. I do not touch your feelings or your heart; my presence causes you neither pleasure nor pain."

"You cannot doubt," she made answer, "that I am glad to see you, and I blush so often when I do see you that you may be sure that the sight of you affects me."

"I am not deceived by your blushes," he urged; "they come from modesty, and not from any thrill of your heart, and I do not exaggerate their importance."

Mademoiselle de Chartres did not know what to answer; these distinctions were outside of her experience. Monsieur de Clèves saw only too well how far removed she was from feeling for him as he should have liked, when he saw that she had no idea of what that feeling was.

The Chevalier de Guise returned from a journey a few days before the wedding.

He had seen so many insurmountable obobstacles in the way of his marrying Mademoiselle de Chartres that he knew he had no chance of success; yet he was evidently distressed at seeing her become the wife of another. This grief did not extinguish his passion, and he remained quite as much in love as before. Mademoiselle de Chartres had not been ignorant of his devotion. On his return he let her know that she was the cause of the deep gloom that marked his face; and he had so much merit and charm that it was almost impossible to make him unhappy without regretting it. Hence she was depressed; but this pity went no further, and she told her mother how much pain this prince's love caused her.

Madame de Chartres admired her daughter's frankness, and with good reason, for it could not be fuller or simpler; she regretted, however, that her heart was not touched, especially when she saw that the prince had not affected it any more than the others.

Hence she took great pains to attach her to her future husband, and to impress upon her what she owed him for the interest he had taken in her before he knew who she was, and for the proof he had given of his love in choosing her at a time when no one else ventured to think of her.

The marriage ceremony took place at the Louvre, and in the evening the king and queen, with all the court, supped at the house of Madame de Chartres, who received them with great splendor. The Chevalier de Guise did not venture to make himself conspicuous by staying away, but his dejection was evident.

Monsieur de Clèves did not find that Mademoiselle de Chartres had altered her feelings when she changed her name. His position as her husband gave him greater privileges, but no different place in her heart. Though he had married her, he did not cease to be her lover, because there was always left something for him to desire; and though she lived on the best of terms with him, he was not yet perfectly happy. He preserved for her a violent and restless passion, which marred his joy. Jealousy had no part in it, for never had a husband been further from feeling it, or a wife from inspiring it. Yet she was exposed to all the temptations of the court, visiting the queen and the king's sister every day. All the young and fashionable men met her at her own house and at that of her brother-in-law, the Duke of Nevers, whose doors were always open; but she always had an air that inspired respect, and seemed so remote from gallantry that the Marshal of Saint-André, though bold and protected by the king's favor, was touched by her beauty without venturing to show it except by delicate attentions. There were many others who felt as did the marshal; and Madame de Chartres added to her daughter's natural modesty such a keen sense of propriety that she made her seem like a woman to be sighed for in vain.

The Duchess of Lorraine, while trying to bring about peace, had also tried to arrange the marriage of her son, the Duke of Lorraine, and had succeeded; he was to marry Madame Claude of France, the king's second daughter. The wedding had been settled for the month of February.

Meanwhile the Duke of Nemours had remained at Brussels, completely taken up with his plans for England. He was always sending and receiving messengers. His hopes grew from day to day, and at last Lignerolles told him that it was time for him to appear and finish in person what had been so well begun. He received this news with all the satisfaction that an ambitious man can feel at seeing himself raised to a throne simply through his reputation. He had gradually grown so accustomed to the contemplation of this great piece of good fortune that whereas at first he had regarded it as an impossibility, all difficulties had vanished, and he foresaw no obstacles.

He at once despatched to Paris orders for a magnificent outfit, that he might make his appearance in England with a splendor proportionate to his designs, and also hastened to court to be present at the wedding of the Duke of Lorraine. He arrived the day before the formal betrothal, and that same evening went to report to the king the condition of affairs and to receive his advice and commands about his future conduct. Thence he went to pay his respects to the queens. Madame de Clèves was not there, so that she did not see him, and was not even aware of his arrival. She had heard every one speak of this prince as the handsomest and most agreeable man at court, and Madame the Dauphiness had spoken of him so often and in such terms that she felt some curiosity to see him.

Madame de Clèves spent the day of the betrothal at home dressing herself for the ball in the evening at the Louvre. When she made her appearance, her beauty and the splendor of her dress aroused general admiration. The ball opened, and while she was dancing with Monsieur de Guise, there was a certain commotion at the door of the ballroom, as if some one were entering for whom way was being made. Madame de Clèves finished her dance, and while she was looking about for another partner, the king called out to her to take the gentleman who had just arrived. She turned, and saw a man, who she thought must be Monsieur de Nemours, stepping over some seats to reach the place where the dancing was going on. No one ever saw this prince for the first time without amazement; and this evening he was more striking than ever in the rich attire which set off his natural beauty to such great advantage; and it was also hard to see Madame de Clèves for the first time without astonishment.

Monsieur de Nemours was so amazed by her beauty that when he drew near her and bowed to her he could not conceal his wonder and delight. When they began their dance, a murmur of admiration ran through the ball-room. The king and the queens remembered that the pair had never met, and saw how strange it was that they should be dancing together without being acquainted. They summoned them when they had finished the set, and without giving them a chance to speak to any one, asked if each would not like to know who the other was, and whether either had any idea.

"As for me, Madame," said Monsieur de Nemours, "I have no doubts; but since Madame de Clèves has not the same reasons for guessing who I am that I have for recognizing her, I must beg your Majesty to be good enough to tell her my name."

"I fancy," said the dauphiness, "that she knows it as well as you know hers."

"I assure you, Madame," said Madame de Clèves, who seemed a little embarrassed, "that I cannot guess so well as you think."

"You can guess very well," replied the dauphiness, "and you are very kind to Monsieur de Nemours in your unwillingness to acknowledge that you recognize him without ever having seen him before."

The queen interrupted the conversation, that the ball might go on, and Monsieur de Nemours danced with the dauphiness. This lady was a perfect beauty, and had always appeared to be one in the eyes of Monsieur de Nemours before he went to Flanders; but all that evening he admired no one but Madame de Clèves.

The Chevalier de Guise, who never ceased worshipping her, was standing near, and this incident caused him evident pain. He regarded it as a sure sign that fate meant that Monsieur de Nemours should fall in love with Madame de Clèves; and whether it was that he saw something in her face, or that jealousy sharpened his fears, he believed that she had been moved by the sight of this prince, and he could not keep from telling her that Monsieur de Nemours was very fortunate in making her acquaintance in such a gallant and unusual way.

Madame de Clèves went home so full of what had happened at the ball that though it was very late, she went to her mother's room to tell her about it; and she praised Monsieur de Nemours with a certain air that made Madame de Chartres entertain the same suspicion as the Chevalier de Guise.

The next day the wedding took place; Madame de Clèves there saw the Duke of Nemours, and was even more struck by his admirable grace and dignity than before.

On succeeding days she met him at the drawing-room of the dauphiness, saw him playing tennis with the king and riding at the ring, and heard him talk; and she always found him so superior to every one else, and so much outshining all in conversation wherever he might be, by the grace of his person and the charm of his wit, that he soon made a deep impression on her heart.

Then, too, the desire to please made the Duke of Nemours, who was already deeply interested, more charming than ever; and since they met often, and found each other more attractive than any one else at court, they naturally experienced great delight in being together.

The Duchess of Valentinois took part in all the merry-making, and the king showed her all the interest and attention that he had done when first in love with her. Madame de Clèves, who was then of an age at which it is usual to believe that no woman can ever be loved after she is twenty-five years old, regarded with great amazement the king's attachment to this duchess, who was a grandmother and had just married her granddaughter. She often spoke of it to Madame de Chartres. "Is it possible," she asked, "that the king has been in love so long? How could he get interested in a woman much older than himself, and who had been his father's mistress, as well as that of a great many other men, as I have heard?"

"It is true," was the answer, "that neither merit nor fidelity inspired the king's passion, or has kept it alive. And this is something which is scarcely to be excused; for had this woman had youth and beauty as well as rank, had she loved no one else, had she loved the king with untiring constancy, for himself alone, and not solely for his wealth and position, and had she used her power for worthy objects such as the king desired, it would have been easy to admire his great devotion to her. If," Madame de Chartres went on, "I were not afraid that you would say of me what is always said of women of my age, that we like to talk about old times, I would tell you the beginning of the king's love for this duchess; and many things that happened at the court of the late king bear much resemblance to what is now going on."

"So far from accusing you of repeating old stories," said Madame de Clèves, "I regret that you have told me so little about the present, and that you have not taught me the different interests and intrigues of the court. I am so ignorant of them that a few days ago I thought the constable was on the best of terms with the queen."

"You were very far from the truth," replied Madame de Chartres. "The queen hates the constable, and if she ever gets any power he will learn it very quickly. She knows that he has often told the king that of all his children it is only his bastards who look like him."

"I should never have imagined this hatred," interrupted Madame de Clèves, "after seeing the zeal with which the queen wrote to the constable when he was in prison, the joy she manifested at his return, and the familiarity of her address as regards him."

"If you judge from appearances here," replied Madame de Chartres, "you will be often mistaken; what appears is seldom the truth.

"But to return to Madame de Valentinois: you know her name is Diane de Poitiers. She is of illustrious family, being descended from the old dukes of Aquitaine; her grandmother was a natural daughter of Louis XI., — in short, there is no common blood in her veins. Saint-Vallier, her father, was implicated in the affair of the Constable of Bourbon, of which you have heard, was condemned to be beheaded, and was led to the scaffold. His daughter, who was remarkably beautiful, and had already pleased the late king, managed, I don't know how, to save her father's life. His pardon was granted him when he was expecting the mortal stroke; but fear had so possessed him that he did not recover consciousness, but died a few days later. His daughter made her appearance at court as the king's mistress. His journey to Italy and his imprisonment interrupted this passion. When he returned from Spain and Madame Régente went to meet him at Bayonne, she had with her all her young women, among whom was Mademoiselle de Pisseleu, afterwards Duchess of Estampes. The king fell in love with her, though she was inferior in birth, beauty, and intelligence to Madame de Valentinois: the only advantage she had was that she was younger. I have often heard her say that she was born on the day that Diane de Potiers was married; but that remark was more malicious than truthful, for I am much mistaken if the Duchess of Valentinois did not marry Monsieur de Brézé, grand seneschal of Normandy, at the same time that the king fell in love with Madame d'Estampes. Never was there fiercer hatred than existed between those two women. The Duchess of Valentinois could not forgive Madame d'Estampes for depriving her of the title of the king's mistress. Madame d'Estampes was madly jealous of Madame de Valentinois because the king maintained his relations with her. This king was never rigorously faithful to his mistresses; there was always one who had the title and the honors, but the ladies of what was called the little band shared his attentions. The death of his oldest son, it was supposed by poison, at Tournon, was a great blow to him. He had much less love for his second son, the present king, who was in every way far less to his taste, and whom he even regarded as lacking courage and spirit. He was lamenting this one day to Madame de Valentinois, whereupon she said she would like to make him fall in love with her, that he might become livelier and more agreeable. She succeeded, as you know. This love has lasted more than twenty years, without being dimmed by time or circumstances.

"At first the late king objected to it, — whether because he was still enough in love with Madame de Valentinois to feel jealous, or because he was influenced by Madame d'Estampes, who was in despair when the dauphin became attached to her enemy, is uncertain; however that may be, he viewed this passion with an anger and a disapproval that were apparent every day. His son feared neither his wrath nor his hate; and since nothing could induce him to abate or to conceal his attachment, the king was forced to endure it as best he could. His son's opposition to his wishes estranged him still more, and attached him more closely to the Duke of Orléans, his third son. This prince was handsome, energetic, ambitious, of a somewhat tempestuous nature, which needed to be controlled, but who in time would become a really fine man.

"The elder son's rank as dauphin and the father's preference for the Duke of Orléans inspired a rivalry between them which amounted to hatred. This rivalry had begun in their childhood, and lasted until the death of the latter. When the emperor entered French territory he gave his whole preference to the Duke of Orléans. This so pained the dauphin that when the emperor was at Chantilly he tried to compel the constable to arrest him, without waiting for the king's orders; but the constable refused. Afterward the king blamed him for not following his son's advice; and this had a good deal to do with his leaving the court.

"The division between the two brothers induced the Duchess of Estampes to rely on the Duke of Orléans for protection against the influence which Madame de Valentinois had over the king. In this she succeeded; the duke, without falling in love with her, was as warm in defence of her interests as was the dauphin in defence of those of Madame de Valentinois. Hence there were two cabals in the court such as you can imagine; but the intrigues were not limited to two women's quarrels.

"The emperor, who had maintained his friendship for the Duke of Orléans, had frequently offered him the duchy of Milan. In the subsequent negotiations about peace, he raised hopes in the breast of the duke that he would give him the seventeen provinces and his daughter's hand. The dauphin, however, desired neither peace nor this marriage. He made use of the constable, whom he has always loved, to convince the king how important it was not to give to his successor a brother so powerful as would be the Duke of Orléans in alliance with the emperor and governing the seventeen provinces. The constable agreed the more heartily with the dauphin's views because he also opposed those of Madame d'Estampes, who was his avowed enemy, and ardently desired that the power of the Duke of Orléans should be increased.

"At that time the dauphin was in command of the king's army in Champagne, and had reduced that of the emperor to such extremities that it would have utterly perished had not the Duchess of Estampes, fearing that too great success would prevent our granting peace and consenting to the marriage, secretly sent word to the enemy to surprise Epernay and Château-Thierry, which were full of supplies. This they did, and thereby saved their whole army.

"This duchess did not long profit by her treason. Soon afterward the Duke of Orléans died at Farmoutier of some contagious disease. He loved one of the most beautiful women of the court, and was beloved by her. I shall not tell you who it was, because her life since that time has been most decorous; and she has tried so hard to have her affection for the prince forgotten that she deserves to have her reputation left untarnished. It so happened that she heard of her husband's death on the same day that she heard of that of Monsieur d'Orléans; consequently she was able to conceal her real grief without an effort.

"The king did not long survive his son's decease, — he died two years later. He urged the dauphin to make use of the services of the Cardinal of Tournon and of the Amiral d'Annebauld, without saying a word about the constable, who at that time was banished to Chantilly. Nevertheless, the first thing the present king did after his father's death was to call the constable back and intrust him with the management of affairs.

"Madame d'Estampes was sent away, and became the victim of all the ill-treatment she might have expected from an all-powerful enemy. The Duchess of Valentinois took full vengeance on this duchess and on all who had displeased her. Her power over the king seemed the greater because it had not appeared while he was dauphin. During the twelve years of his reign she has been in everything absolute mistress. She disposes of places and controls affairs of every sort; she secured the dismissal of the Cardinal of Tournon, of the Chancelier Olivier, and of Villeroy. Those who have endeavored to open the king's eyes to her conduct have been ruined for their pains. The Count of Taix, commander-in-chief of the artillery, who did not like her, could not keep from talking about her love affairs, and especially about one with the Count of Brissac, of whom the king was already very jealous. Yet she managed so well that the Count of Taix was disgraced and deprived of his position; and impossible as it may sound, he was succeeded by the Count of Brissac, whom she afterward made a marshal of France. Still, the king's jealousy became so violent that he could not endure having this marshal remain at court; but though usually jealousy is a hot and violent passion, it is modified and tempered in him by his extreme respect for his mistress, so that the only means he ventured to use to rid himself of his rival was by intrusting to him the government of Piedmont. There he has spent several years; last winter, however, he returned, under the pretext of asking for men and supplies for the army under his command. Possibly the desire of seeing Madame de Valentinois and dread of being forgotten had something to do with this journey. The king received

him very coldly. The Guises, who do not
like him, did not dare betray their feelings,
on account of Madame de Valentinois, so
they made use of the Vidame, his open
enemy, to prevent his getting any of the
things he wanted. It was not hard to injure
him. The king hated him, and was made
uneasy by his presence; consequently he
was obliged to go back without getting
any advantage from his journey, — unless,
possibly, he had rekindled in the heart of
Madame de Valentinois feelings which absence had nearly extinguished. The king
has had many other grounds for jealousy,
but either he has not known them, or he
has not dared to complain.

"I am not sure, my dear," added Madame
de Chartres, "that you may not think I have
told you more than you cared to hear."

"Not at all," answered Madame de Clèves;
"and if I were not afraid of tiring you, I
should ask you many more questions."

Monsieur de Nemours' love for Madame de

Clèves was at first so violent that he lost all interest in those he had formerly loved, and with whom he had kept up relations during his absence. He not merely did not seek any excuses for deserting them, he would not even listen to their complaints or reply to their reproaches. The dauphiness, for whom he had nourished very warm feelings, was soon forgotten by the side of Madame de Clèves. His impatience for his journey to England began to abate, and he ceased to hasten his preparations for departure. He often visited the crown princess, because Madame de Clèves was frequently in her apartments, and he was not unwilling to give some justification to the widespread suspicions about his feelings for the dauphiness. Madame de Clèves seemed to him so rare a prize that he decided to conceal all signs of his love rather than let it be generally known. He never spoke of it even to his intimate friend the Vidame de Chartres, to whom he usually confided everything. He was so cautious and discreet that no one suspected his love for Madame de Clèves except the Chevalier de Guise; and the lady herself would scarcely have perceived it had not her own interest in him made her watch him very closely, so that she became sure of it.

Madame de Clèves did not find herself so disposed to tell her mother what she thought of this prince's feelings as had been the case with her other lovers; and without definitely deciding on reserve, she yet never spoke of the subject. But Madame de Chartres soon perceived this, as well as her daughter's interest in him. This knowledge gave her distinct pain, for she well understood how dangerous it was for Madame de Clèves to be loved by a man like Monsieur de Nemours, especially when she was already disposed to admire him. An incident that happened a few days later confirmed her suspicions of this liking.

The Marshal of Saint-André, who was

always on the look-out for opportunities to display his magnificence, made a pretext of desiring to show his house, which had just been finished, and invited the king to do him the honor of supping there with the queens. The marshal was also glad to be able to show to Madame de Clèves his lavish splendor.

A few days before the one of the supper, the dauphin, whose health was delicate, had been ailing and had seen no one. His wife, the crown princess, had spent the whole day with him, and toward evening, as he felt better, he received all the persons of quality who were in his ante-chamber. The crown princess went to her own apartment, where she found Madame de Clèves and a few other ladies with whom she was most intimate.

Since it was already late, and the crown princess was not dressed, she did not go to the queen, but sent word she could not come; she then had her jewels brought, to decide what she should wear at the Marshal of Saint-André's ball, and to give some, according to a promise she had made, to Madame de Clèves. While they were thus occupied, the Prince of Condé, whose rank gave him free admission everywhere, entered. The crown princess said to him that he doubtless came from her husband, and asked what was going on in his apartments.

"They are having a discussion, Madame, with Monsieur de Nemours," he answered. "He defends the side he has taken so eagerly that he must have a personal interest in it. I fancy he has a mistress who makes him uneasy when she goes to a ball, for he maintains that it makes a lover unhappy to see the woman he loves at such a place."

"What!" said the dauphiness, "Monsieur de Nemours does not want his mistress to go to a ball? I thought husbands might object, but I never supposed that lovers could have such a feeling."

"Monsieur de Nemours," replied the Prince

of Condé, " declares that a ball is most distressing to lovers, whether they are loved or not. He says if their love is returned, they have the pain of being loved less for several days; that there is not a woman in the world who is not prevented from thinking of her lover by the demands of her toilet, which entirely engrosses her attention; that women dress for every one as well as for those they love; that when they are at the ball they are anxious to please all who look at them; that when they are proud of their beauty, they feel a pleasure in which the lover plays but a small part. He says, too, that one who sighs in vain suffers even more when he sees his mistress at an entertainment; that the more she is admired by the public, the more one suffers at not being loved, through fear lest her beauty should kindle some love happier than his own; finally, that there is no pain so keen as seeing one's mistress at a ball, except knowing that she is there while absent one's self."

Madame de Clèves, though pretending not to hear what the Prince of Condé was saying, listened attentively. She readily understood her share in the opinion expressed by Monsieur de Nemours, especially when he spoke of his grief at not being at the ball with his mistress, because he was not to be at that given by the Marshal of Saint-André, being ordered by the king to go to meet the Duke of Ferrara.

The crown princess laughed with the Prince of Condé, and expressed her disapproval of the views of Monsieur de Nemours. "There is only one condition, Madame," said the prince, "on which Monsieur de Nemours is willing that his mistress should go to a ball, and that is that he himself should give her permission. He said that last year when he gave a ball to your Majesty, he thought that his mistress did him a great favor in coming to it, though she seemed to be there only as one of your suite; that it is always a kindness to a lover to take part in any entertainment that he gives; and that it is also agreeable to a lover to have his mistress see him the host of the whole court and doing the honors fittingly."

"Monsieur de Nemours did well," said the dauphiness, with a smile, "to let his mistress go to that ball; for so many women claimed that position that if they had not come, there would have been scarcely any one there."

As soon as the Prince of Condé had begun to speak of what Monsieur de Nemours thought of the ball, Madame de Clèves was very anxious not to go to that of the Marshal of Saint-André. She readily agreed that it was not fitting for a woman to go to the house of a man who was in love with her, and she was glad to have so good a reason for doing a kindness to Monsieur de Nemours. Nevertheless, she took away the jewels which the crown princess had given her; that evening, however, when she showed them to her mother, she told her that she did not mean to wear them, that the Marshal of

Saint-André had made his love for her so manifest that she felt sure he meant to have it thought that she was to have some part in the entertainment he was to give to the king, and that under the pretext of doing honor to the king he would pay her attentions which might perhaps prove embarrassing.

Madame de Chartres argued for some time against her daughter's decision, which she thought singular, but at last yielded, and told her she must pretend to be ill, in order to have a good excuse for not going, because her real reasons would not be approved and should not be suspected. Madame de Clèves gladly consented to stay at home for a few days, in order not to meet Monsieur de Nemours, who left without having the pleasure of knowing that she was not going to the ball.

The duke returned the day after the ball, and heard that she had not been there; but inasmuch as he did not know that his talk with the dauphin had been repeated to her, he was far from thinking that he was fortunate enough to be the cause of her absence.

The next day, when Monsieur de Nemours was calling on the queen and talking with the dauphiness, Madame de Chartres and Madame de Clèves happened to come in and approached this princess. Madame de Clèves was not in full dress, as if she were not very well, though her countenance belied her attire.

"You look so well," said the crown princess, "that I can scarcely believe that you have been ill. I fancy that the Prince of Condé, when he told you what Monsieur de Nemours thought about the ball, convinced you that you would do a kindness to the Marshal of Saint-André by going to his ball, and that that was the reason you stayed away."

Madame de Clèves blushed at the dauphiness's accurate guess which she thus expressed before Monsieur de Nemours.

Madame de Chartres saw at once why her daughter did not go to the ball, and in order to throw Monsieur de Nemours off the track, she at once addressed the dauphiness with an air of sincerity. "I assure you, Madame," she said, "that your Majesty pays an honor to my daughter which she does not deserve. She was really ill; but I am sure that if I had not forbidden it, she would have accompanied you, unfit as she was, to have the pleasure of seeing the wonderful entertainment last evening."

The dauphiness believed what Madame de Chartres said, and Monsieur de Nemours was vexed to see how probable her story was; nevertheless the confusion of Madame de Clèves made him suspect that the dauphiness's conjecture was not without some foundation in fact. At first Madame de Clèves had been annoyed because Monsieur de Nemours had reason to suppose that it was he who had kept her from going to the ball, and then she felt regret that her mother had entirely removed the grounds for this supposition.

Although the attempt to make peace at Cercamp had failed, negotiations still continued, and matters had assumed such a shape that toward the end of February a meeting was held at Câteau-Cambresis. The same commissioners had assembled there, and the departure of the Marshal of Saint-André freed Monsieur de Nemours from a rival who was more to be dreaded on account of his close observation of all those who approached Madame de Clèves than from any real success of his own.

Madame de Chartres did not wish to let her daughter see that she knew her feeling for this prince, lest she should make her suspicious of the advice she wanted to give her. One day she began to talk about him. She spoke of him in warm terms, but craftily praised his discretion in being unable to fall really in love and in seeking only pleasure, not a serious attachment, in his relations with women. "To be sure," she went on, "he has been suspected of a great passion for the dauphiness; I notice that he visits her very often, and I advise you to avoid talking with him as much as possible, especially in private, because you are on such terms with the crown princess that people would say that you were their confidant, and you know how disagreeable that would be. I think that if the report continues, you would do well to see less of the crown princess, that you may not be connected with love-affairs of that sort."

Madame de Clèves had never heard Monsieur de Nemours and the dauphiness talked about, and was much surprised by what her mother said. She was so sure that she had misunderstood the prince's feelings for her that she changed color. Madame de Chartres noticed this, but company coming in at that moment, Madame de Clèves went home and locked herself up in her room.

It is impossible to express her grief when

her mother's words opened her eyes to the interest she took in Monsieur de Nemours; she had never dared to acknowledge it to herself. Then she saw that her feelings for him were what Monsieur de Clèves had so often supplicated, and she felt the mortification of having them for another than a husband who so well deserved them. She felt hurt and embarrassed, fearing that Monsieur de Nemours might have used her as a pretext for seeing the dauphiness; and this thought decided her to tell Madame de Chartres what she had hitherto kept secret.

The next morning she went to her mother to carry out this decision; but Madame de Chartres was a little feverish, and did not care to talk with her. The illness seemed so slight, however, that Madame de Clèves called on the dauphiness after dinner, and found her in her room with two or three ladies with whom she was on intimate terms.

"We were talking about Monsieur de Nemours," said the queen when she saw her, "and were surprised to see how much he is changed since his return from Brussels; before he went, he had an infinite number of mistresses, and it was a positive disadvantage to him, because he used to be kind both to those who were worthy and to those who were not. Since his return, however, he will have nothing to do with any of them. There has never been such a change. His spirits, moreover, seem to be affected, as he is much less cheerful than usual."

Madame de Clèves made no answer; she thought with a sense of shame that she would have taken all that they said about the change in him for a proof of his passion if she had not been undeceived. She was somewhat vexed with the dauphiness for trying to explain and for expressing surprise at something of which she must know the real reason better than any one else. She could not keep from showing her annoyance, and when the other ladies withdrew, she went up to the crown princess and said in a low voice, —

"Is it for my benefit that you have just spoken, and do you want to hide from me that you are the cause of the altered conduct of Monsieur de Nemours?"

"You are unjust," said the crown princess; "you know that I never keep anything from you. It is true that before he went to Brussels, Monsieur de Nemours meant to have me understand that he did not hate me; but since his return he seems to have forgotten all about it, and I confess that I am a little curious about the reason of this change. I shall probably find it out," she went on, "as the Vidame de Chartres, his intimate friend, is in love with a young woman over whom I have some power, and I shall know from her what has made this change."

The dauphiness spoke with an air that

carried conviction to Madame de Clèves, who found herself calmer and happier than she had been before. When she went back to her mother, she found her much worse than when she had left her. She was more feverish, and for some days it seemed as if she were going to be really ill. Madame de Clèves was in great distress, and did not leave her mother's room. Monsieur de Clèves spent nearly all his time there too, both to comfort his wife and to have the pleasure of seeing her: his love had not lessened.

Monsieur de Nemours, who had always been one of his friends, had not neglected him since his return from Brussels. During the illness of Madame de Chartres he found it possible to see Madame de Clèves very often, under pretence of calling on her husband or of stopping to take him to walk. He even sought him at hours when he knew he was not in; then he would say that he would wait for him, and used to stay in the ante-chamber of Madame de Chartres, where were assembled many persons of quality. Madame de Clèves would often look in, and although she was in great anxiety, she seemed no less beautiful to Monsieur de Nemours. He showed her how much he sympathized with her distress, and soon convinced her that it was not with the dauphiness that he was in love.

She could not keep from being embarrassed, and yet delighted to see him; but when he was out of her sight and she remembered that this pleasure was the beginning of an unhappy passion, she felt she almost hated him, so much did the idea of guilty love pain her.

Madame de Chartres rapidly grew worse, and soon her life was despaired of; she heard the doctors' opinion of her danger with a courage proportionate to her virtue and piety. After they had left her, she dismissed all who were present, and sent for Madame de Clèves.

"We have to part, my daughter," she said, holding out her hand; "and the peril in which you are and the need you have of me, double my pain in leaving you. You have an affection for Monsieur de Nemours; I do not ask you to confess it, as I am no longer able to make use of your sincerity in order to guide you. It is long since I perceived this affection, but I have been averse to speaking to you about it, lest you should become aware of it yourself. Now you know it only too well. You are on the edge of a precipice: a great effort, a violent struggle, alone can save you. Think of what you owe your husband, think of what you owe yourself, and remember that you are in danger of losing that reputation which you have acquired and which I have so ardently desired for you. Take strength and courage, my daughter: withdraw from the court; compel your husband to take you away. Do not be afraid of making a difficult decision. Terrible as it may appear at first, it will in the end be pleasanter than the consequences of a love-affair. If any other reasons than virtue and duty can persuade you to what I wish, let me say that if anything is capable of destroying the happiness I hope for in another world, it would be seeing you fall like so many women; but if this misfortune must come to you, I welcome death that I may not see it."

Madame de Clèves's tears fell on her mother's hand, which she held clasped in her own, and Madame de Chartres saw that she was moved. "Good-by, my daughter," she said; "let us put an end to a conversation which moves us both too deeply, and remember, if you can, all I have just said to you."

With these words she turned away and bade her daughter call her women, without hearing or saying more. Madame de Clèves left her mother's room in a state that may be imagined, and Madame de Chartres thought of nothing but preparing herself for death. She lingered two days more, but refused again to see her daughter, — the only person she loved.

Madame de Clèves was in sore distress; her husband never left her side, and as soon as Madame de Chartres had died, he took her into the country, to get her away from a place which continually renewed her grief, which was intense. Although her love and gratitude to her mother counted for a great deal, the need she felt of her support against Monsieur de Nemours made the blow even more painful. She lamented being left to herself when she had her emotions so little under control, and when she so needed some one to pity her and give her strength. Her husband's kindness made her wish more than ever to be always true to him. She showed him more affection and kindliness than she had ever done before, and she wanted him always by her side; for it seemed to her that her attachment to him would prove a defence against Monsieur de Nemours.

This prince went to visit Monsieur de Clèves in the country, and did his best to see Madame de Clèves; but she declined to receive him, knowing that she could not fail to find him charming. Moreover, she resolutely determined to avoid every occasion of meeting him, so far as she was able.

Monsieur de Clèves repaired to Paris to pay his respects at court, promising his wife to return the next day; but he did not return till the day after.

"I expected you all day yesterday," Madame de Clèves said to him when he arrived, "and I ought to find fault with you for not returning when you promised. You know that if I could feel a new sorrow in the state I am in, it would be at the death of Madame de Tournon, of which I heard this morning. I should have been distressed by it even if I had not known her. It is always painful when a young and beautiful woman like her dies after an illness of only two days, and much more so when it is one of the persons I liked best in the world, and who seemed as modest as she was worthy."

"I was sorry not to return yesterday," answered Monsieur de Clèves; "but it was so imperatively necessary that I should console an unhappy man that I could not possibly leave him. As for Madame de Tournon, I advise you not to be too profoundly distressed, if you mourn her as an upright woman who deserved your esteem."

"You surprise me," said Madame de Clèves, "as I have often heard you say that there was no woman at court whom you esteemed more highly."

"That is true," he answered; "but women

are incomprehensible, and the more I see of them, the happier I feel that I have married you, and I cannot be sufficiently grateful for my good fortune."

"You think better of me than I deserve," exclaimed Madame de Clèves, with a sigh, "and it is much too soon to think me worthy of you. But tell me, please, what has undeceived you about Madame de Tournon."

"I have long been undeceived in regard to her," he replied, "and have long known that she loved the Count of Sancerre, to whom she held out hopes that she would marry him."

"I can scarcely believe," interrupted Madame de Clèves, "that Madame de Tournon, after the extraordinary reluctance to matrimony which she showed after she became a widow, and after her public assertions that she would never marry again, should have given Sancerre any hopes."

"If she had given them only to him," replied Monsieur de Clèves, "there would be little occasion for surprise; but what is astounding is that she also gave them to Estouteville at the same time, and I will tell you the whole story."

PART II.

"YOU know," Monsieur de Clèves continued, "what good friends Sancerre and I are; yet when, about two years ago, he fell in love with Madame de Tournon, he took great pains to conceal it from me, as well as from every one else, and I was far from suspecting it. Madame de Tournon appeared still inconsolable for her husband's death, and was still living in the most absolute retirement. Sancerre's sister was almost the only person she saw, and it was at her house that the count fell in love with her.

"One evening when there was to be a play at the Louvre, and while they were waiting for the king and Madame de Valentinois in order to begin, word was brought that she was ill and that the king would not come. Every one guessed that the duchess's illness was some quarrel with the king. We knew how jealous he had been of the Marshal of Brissac during his stay at court; but the marshal had gone back to Piedmont a few days before, and we could not imagine the cause of this falling-out.

"While I was talking about it with Sancerre, Monsieur d'Anville came into the hall and whispered to me that the king was in a state of distress and anger most piteous to see; that when he and Madame de Valentinois were reconciled a few days before, after their quarrels about the Marshal of Brissac, the king had given her a ring and asked her to wear it. While she was dressing for the play, he had noticed its absence, and had asked her the reason. She seemed surprised to miss it, and asked her women for it; but they, unfortunately, perhaps because they had not been put on their guard, said that it was some four or five days since they had seen it.

"' That exactly corresponded with the date of the Marshal of Brissac's departure,' Monsieur d'Anville went on; 'and the king is convinced that she gave him the ring when she bade him good-by. This thought has so aroused all his jealousy, which was by no means wholly extinguished, that, contrary to his usual custom, he flew into a rage and reproached her bitterly. He has gone back to his room in great distress, whether because he thinks that Madame de Valentinois has given away his ring, or because he fears that he has displeased her by his wrath, I do not know.'

"As soon as Monsieur d'Anville had finished, I went up to Sancerre to tell him the news, assuring him that it was a secret that had just been told me, and was to go no farther.

"The next morning I called rather early on my sister-in-law, and found Madame de Tournon there. She did not like Madame de Valentinois, and knew very well that my sister-in-law also had no reason for being fond of her. Sancerre had seen her when he left the play, and had told her about the king's quarrel with the duchess; this she had come to repeat to my sister-in-law, either not knowing or not remembering that it was I who had told her lover.

"When I came in, my sister-in-law said to Madame de Tournon that I could be trusted with what she had just told her, and without waiting for permission she repeated to me word for word everything I had told Sancerre the previous evening. You will understand my surprise. I looked at Madame de Tournon, who seemed embarrassed, and her embarrassment aroused my suspicions. I had mentioned the matter to no one but Sancerre, who had left me after the play, without saying where he was going; but

I remembered hearing him praise Madame de Tournon very warmly. All these things opened my eyes, and I soon decided that there was a love-affair between them, and that he had seen her after he left me.

"I was so annoyed to find that he kept the matter secret from me that I said a good many things that made it clear to Madame de Tournon that she had been imprudent; as I handed her to her carriage, I assured her that I envied the happiness of the person who had informed her of the falling-out of the king and Madame de Valentinois.

"At once I went to see Sancerre; I reproached him, and said that I knew of his passion for Madame de Tournon, but I did not say how I had found it out. He felt obliged to make a complete confession. I then told him how it was I had discovered his secret, and he told me all about the affair; he said that inasmuch as he was a younger son, and far from having any claims to such an honor, she was yet determined to marry

him. No one could be more surprised than
I was. I urged Sancerre to hasten his marriage, and told him that he would be justified
in fearing anything from a woman who was
so full of craft that she could play so false a
part before the public. He said in reply that
her grief had been sincere, but that it had
yielded before her affection for him, and
that she could not suddenly make this great
change manifest. He brought up many
other things in her defence, which showed
me clearly how much in love he was; he
assured me that he would persuade her to
let me know all about the passion he had
for her, since it was she who had let out the
secret, — and in fact he compelled her to
consent, though with much difficulty, and I
was from that time fully admitted to their
confidence.

"I have never seen a woman so honorable
and agreeable toward her lover; yet I was
always pained by her affectation of grief.
Sancerre was so much in love, and so well

satisfied with the way she treated him, that he was almost afraid to urge their marriage, lest she should think that he was moved thereto by interest rather than passion. Still, he often talked to her about it, and she seemed to have decided to marry him; she even began to leave her retirement and to reappear in the world, — she used to come to my sister-in-law's at the time when part of the court used to be there. Sancerre came very seldom; but those who were there every evening and met her often, found her very charming.

"Shortly after she began to come out again into society, Sancerre imagined that he detected some coolness in her love for him. He spoke to me about it several times without rousing any anxiety in me by his complaints; but when at length he told me that instead of hastening, she seemed to be postponing their marriage, I began to think that he had good grounds for uneasiness. I said that even if Madame de Tournon's passion should lessen after lasting for two years, he ought not to be surprised; that even if it did not lessen, and though it should not be strong enough to persuade her to marry him, he ought not to complain; since their marriage would injure her much in the eyes of the public, not only because he was not a very good match for her, but because it would affect her reputation: hence that all he could reasonably desire was that she should not deceive him and feed him with false hopes. I also said that if she had not the courage to marry him, or if she should confess that she loved some one else, he ought not to be angry or complain, but preserve his esteem and gratitude for her.

"'I give you the advice,' I said to him, 'which I should take myself; for I am so touched by sincerity that I believe that if my mistress, or my wife, were to confess that any one pleased her, I should be distressed without being angered, and should lay aside the character of lover or husband to advise and sympathize with her.'"

At these words Madame de Clèves blushed, finding a certain likeness to her own condition which surprised her and distressed her for some time.

"Sancerre spoke to Madame de Tournon," Monsieur de Clèves went on, "telling her everything I had advised; but she reassured him with such tact and seemed so pained by his suspicions that she entirely dispelled them. Nevertheless she postponed their marriage until after a long journey which he was about to make; but her conduct was so discreet up to the time of his departure, and she seemed so grieved at parting with him, that I, as well as he, believed that she truly loved him. He went away about three months ago. During his absence I saw Madame de Tournon very seldom; you have taken up all my time, and I only knew that Sancerre was to return soon.

"The day before yesterday, on my arrival

in Paris, I heard that she was dead. I at once sent to his house to find out if they had heard from him, and was told that he had arrived the day before, — the very day of Madame de Tournon's death. I went at once to see him, knowing very well in what a state I should find him; but his agony far exceeded what I had imagined. Never have I seen such deep and tender grief. As soon as he saw me, he embraced me, bursting into tears. 'I shall never see her again,' he said, 'I shall never see her again; she is dead! I was not worthy of her; but I shall soon follow her.'

"After that he was silent; then from time to time he repeated: 'She is dead, and I shall never see her again!' Thereupon he would again burst into tears, and seemed out of his head. He told me he had received but few letters from her while away, but that this did not surprise him, because he well knew her aversion to running any risk in writing letters. He had no doubt that she would have married him on his return; and he looked upon her as the most amiable and faithful woman who had ever lived; he believed that she loved him tenderly, and that he had lost her at the moment when he made sure of winning her forever. These thoughts plunged him into the deepest distress, by which he was wholly overcome, and I confess that I was deeply moved.

"Nevertheless, I was obliged to leave him to go to the king, but I promised to return soon. This I did; but imagine my surprise when I found that he was in an entirely different mood. He was pacing up and down his room with a wild face, and he stopped as if he were beside himself and said: 'Come, come! see the most desperate man in the world; I am ten thousand times unhappier than I was before, and what I have just heard of Madame de Tournon is worse than her death.'

"I thought that his grief had crazed him, for I could imagine nothing more terrible than the death of a loved mistress who returns one's love. I told him that so long as his grief had been within bounds I had understood and sympathized with it; but that I should cease to pity him if he gave way to despair and lost his mind. 'I wish I could lose it, and my life too,' he exclaimed. 'Madame de Tournon was unfaithful to me; and I ascertained her infidelity and treachery the day after I heard of her death, at a time when my soul was filled with the deepest grief and the tenderest love that were ever felt, — at a time when my heart was filled with the thought of her as the most perfect creature that had ever lived, and the most generous to me. I find that I was mistaken in her, and that she does not deserve my tears; nevertheless, I have the same grief from her death as if she had been faithful to me, and I suffer from her infidelity as if she were not dead. Had I known of her changed feeling before she died, I should have been wild with wrath and jealousy, and should have been in some way hardened against the blow of her death; but now I can get no consolation from it or hate her.'

"You may judge of my surprise at what Sancerre told me; I asked him how he found this out. He told me that the moment I had left his room, Estouteville, an intimate friend of his, though he knew nothing of his love for Madame de Tournon, had come to see him; that as soon as he had sat down, he burst into tears and said he begged his pardon for not having told him before what he was about to say; that he begged him to take pity on him; that he had come to open his heart to him; and that he saw before him a man utterly crushed by the death of Madame de Tournon.

"'That name,' said Sancerre, 'surprised me so that my first impulse was to tell him that I was much more distressed than he; but I was unable to speak a word. He went on and told me that he had been in love with her for six months; that he had always

meant to tell me, but she had forbidden it
so firmly that he had not dared to disobey
her; that almost ever since he fell in love
with her she had taken a tender interest in
him; that he only visited her secretly; that
he had had the pleasure of consoling her for
the loss of her husband; and, finally, that he
was on the point of marrying her at the time
of her death, but that this marriage, which
would have been one of love, would have
appeared to be one of duty and obedience,
because she had won over her father to command this marriage, in order that there
should not be any great change in her conduct, which had indicated an unwillingness
to contract a second marriage.

"'While Estouteville was speaking,' Sancerre went on, 'I fully believed him, because
what he said seemed likely, and the time he
had mentioned as that when he fell in love with
Madame de Tournon coincided with that of
her altered treatment of me. But a moment
after, I thought him a liar, or at least out of

his senses, and I was ready to tell him so. I thought, however, I would first make sure; hence I began to question him and to show that I had my doubts. At last I was so persistent in the search of my unhappiness that he asked if I knew Madame de Tournon's handwriting, and placed on my bed four of her letters and her portrait. My brother happened to come in at that moment. Estouteville's face was so stained with tears that he had to go away in order not to be seen in that state; he told me that he would come back that evening to get the things he left. I sent my brother away, pretending that I was not feeling well, being impatient to read the letters, and still hoping to find something which would convince me that Estouteville was mistaken. But, alas, what did I not find! What tenderness, what protestations, what promises to marry him, what letters! She had never written me any like them. So,' he went on, 'I suffer at the same time grief for her death and for her faithlessness, — two misfortunes which have often been compared, but have never been felt at the same time by one person. I confess, to my shame, that I feel much more keenly her death than her change; I cannot find her guilty enough to deserve to die. If she were still alive, I should have the pleasure of reproaching her, of avenging myself by showing her how great was her injustice. But I shall never see her again.' He repeated, 'I shall never see her again, — that is the bitterest blow of all; I would gladly give up my life for hers. What a wish! If she were to return, she would live for Estouteville. How happy I was yesterday!' he exclaimed, 'how happy I was then! I was the most sorely distressed man in the world; but my distress was in the order of nature, and I drew some comfort from the thought that I could never be consoled. To-day all my feelings are false ones; I pay to the pretended love she felt for me the same tribute that

I thought due to a real affection. I can neither hate nor love her memory; I am incapable of consolation or of grief. At least,' he said, turning suddenly toward me, 'let me, I beg of you, never see Estouteville again; his very name fills me with horror. I know very well that I have no reason to blame him; it is my own fault for concealing from him my love for Madame de Tournon: if he had known of it, he would perhaps have never cared for her, and she would not have been unfaithful to me. He came to see me to confide his grief; I really pity him. Yes, and with good reason,' he exclaimed; 'he loved Madame de Tournon and was loved by her. He will never see her again; yet I feel that I cannot keep from hating him. Once more, I beg of you never to let me see him again.'

"Thereupon Sancerre burst again into tears, mourning Madame de Tournon, saying to her the tenderest things imaginable; thence he changed to hatred, complaints, reproaches, and denunciations of her conduct. When I saw him in this desperate state I knew that I should need some aid in calming him, so I sent for his brother, whom I had just left with the king. I went out to speak to him in the hall before he came in, and I told him what a state Sancerre was in. We gave orders that he was not to see Estouteville, and spent a good part of the night trying to persuade him to listen to reason. This morning I found him in still deeper distress; his brother is staying with him, and I have returned to you."

"No one could be more surprised than I am," said Madame de Clèves, "for I thought Madame de Tournon incapable of both love and deception."

"Address and dissimulation," answered Monsieur de Clèves, "could not go further. Notice that when Sancerre thought she had changed toward him, she really had, and had begun to love Estouteville. She told her new lover that he consoled her for her husband's death, and that it was he who was the cause of her returning to society; while it seemed to Sancerre that it was because we had decided that she should no longer appear to be in such deep affliction. She was able to persuade Estouteville to conceal their relations, and to seem obliged to marry him by her father's orders, as if it were the result of her care for her reputation, — and this in order to abandon Sancerre without leaving him ground for complaint. I must go back," continued Monsieur de Clèves, "to see this unhappy man, and I think you had better return to Paris. It is time for you to see company and to begin to receive the number of visits that await you."

Madame de Clèves gave her consent, and they returned the next day. She found herself more tranquil about Monsieur de Nemours than she had been; Madame de Chartres' dying words and her deep grief had for a time dulled her feelings, and she thought they had entirely changed.

The evening of Madame de Clèves's arrival the dauphiness came to see her, and after expressing her sympathy with her affliction, said that in order to drive away her sad thoughts she would tell her everything that had taken place at court during her absence, and narrated many incidents. "But what I most want to tell you," she added, "is that it is certain that Monsieur de Nemours is passionately in love, and that his most intimate friends are not only not in his confidence, but they can't even guess whom it is whom he loves. Yet this love is strong enough to make him neglect, or rather give up, the hope of a crown."

The dauphiness then told Madame de Clèves the whole plan about England. "I heard what I have just told you," she went on, "from Monsieur d'Anville; and he said to me this morning that the king sent last evening for Monsieur de Nemours, after reading some letters from Lignerolles, who is anxious to return, and had written to the king that he was unable to explain to the Queen of England Monsieur de Nemours' delay; that she is beginning to be offended; and that although she has given no positive answer, she had said enough to warrant him in starting. The king read this letter to Monsieur de Nemours, who instead of talking seriously, as he had done in the beginning, only laughed and joked about Lignerolles' hopes. He said that the whole of Europe would blame his imprudence if he were to presume to go to England as a claimant for the queen's hand without being assured of success. 'It seems to me too,' he went on, 'that I should not choose the present time for my journey, when the King of Spain is doing his best to marry her. In a love-affair he would not be a very formidable rival; but I think that in a question of marrying, your Majesty would not advise me to try my chances against him.' 'I do advise you so in the present circumstances,' answered the king.

'But you have no occasion to fear him. I know that he has other thoughts, and even if he had not, Queen Mary was too unhappy under the Spanish yoke for one to believe that her sister wishes to assume it, or would let herself be dazzled by the splendor of so many united crowns.' 'If she does not let herself be dazzled by them,' went on Monsieur de Nemours, ' probably she will wish to marry for love; she has loved Lord Courtenay for several years. Queen Mary also loved him, and she would have married him, with the consent of the whole of England, had she not known that the youth and beauty of her sister Elizabeth attracted him more than the desire of reigning. Your Majesty knows that her violent jealousy caused her to throw them both into prison, then to exile Lord Courtenay, and finally decided her to marry the King of Spain. I believe that Elizabeth, now that she is on the throne, will soon recall this lord and thus choose a man she has loved, who is very attractive, and who has suffered so much for her, rather than another whom she has never seen.' 'I should agree with you,' replied the king, 'if Courtenay were still living; but some days ago I heard that he had died at Padua, where he was living in banishment. I see very well,' he added, as he left Monsieur de Nemours, 'that it will be necessary to celebrate your marriage as we should celebrate the dauphin's, by sending ambassadors to marry the Queen of England by procuration.'

"Monsieur d'Anville and the Vidame, who were present while the king was talking with Monsieur de Nemours, are convinced that it is this great passion which has dissuaded him from this plan. The Vidame, who is more intimate than any one with him, said to Madame de Martigues that the prince is changed beyond recognition; and what amazes him still more is that he never finds him engaged or absent, so that he supposes he never meets the woman he loves; and what is so surprising, is to see Monsieur de Nemours in love with a woman who does not return his passion."

All this story that the dauphiness told her was as poison to Madame de Clèves. It was impossible for her not to feel sure that she was the woman whose name was unknown; and she was overwhelmed with gratitude and tenderness when she learned from one who had the best means of knowing that this prince, who had already aroused her interest, hid his passion from every one, and for love of her gave up his chances of a crown. It is impossible to describe her agitation. If the dauphiness had observed her with any care, she would at once have seen that the story she had just repeated was by no means without interest to her; but having no suspicion of the truth, she went on without noticing her. "Monsieur d'Anville," she added, "who, as I said, told me all this, thinks that I know more about it than he does, and he has so high an opinion of my charms that he is convinced that I am the only person who can make such a great change in Monsieur de Nemours."

Madame de Clèves was agitated by this last remark of the crown princess, though not in the same way as a few moments before. "I should readily agree with Monsieur d'Anville," she replied, "and it is certainly probable, Madame, that no one but a princess like you could make him indifferent to the Queen of England."

"I should at once acknowledge it," said the dauphiness, "if I knew that was the case, and I should know if it were true. Love-affairs of that sort do not escape the notice of those who inspire them; they are the first to perceive them. Monsieur de Nemours has never paid any but the most insignificant attentions; but there is nevertheless so great a difference between his way with me and his present conduct that I can assure you I am not the cause of the indifference he shows for the crown of England.

"I forget everything while I am with you," she went on, "and it had slipped my mind that I must go to see Madame Elisabeth. You know that peace is nearly concluded; but what you don't know is that the King of Spain would not agree to a single article except on the condition that he, instead of the prince Don Carlos, his son, should marry this princess. The king had great difficulty in agreeing to this; at last he yielded, and has gone to tell Madame. I fancy she will be inconsolable; it certainly cannot be pleasant to marry a man of the age and temper of the King of Spain, especially for her, who, in all the pride of youth and beauty, expected to marry a young prince for whom she has a fancy, though she has never seen him. I don't know whether the king will find her as docile as he wishes, and he has asked me to go to see her; for he knows that she is fond of me, and imagines that I have some influence over her. I shall then make a very different visit, for I must go to congratulate Madame, the king's sister. Everything is arranged for her marriage with Monsieur de Savoie, and he will be here shortly. Never was a person of the age of that princess so glad to marry. The court will be finer and larger than it has ever been, and in spite of your afflictions you must come and help us show the foreigners that we have some famous beauties here."

Then the dauphiness left Madame de Clèves, and the next day Madame Elisabeth's marriage was known to every one. A few days later the king and the queens called on Madame de Clèves. Monsieur de Nemours, who had awaited her return with extreme impatience, and was very desirous of speaking to her alone, put off his call until every one should have left and it was unlikely that others would come in. His plan was successful, and he arrived just as the latest visitors were taking their departure.

The princess was still lying down; it was warm, and the sight of Monsieur de Nemours gave her face an additional color, which did not lessen her beauty. He sat down opposite her with the timidity and shyness that real passion gives. It was some time before he spoke; Madame de Clèves was equally confused, so that they kept a long silence. At last Monsieur de Nemours took courage, and expressed his sympathy with her grief. Madame de Clèves, who was glad to keep the conversation on this safe topic, spoke for some time about the loss she had experienced; and finally she said that when time should have dimmed the intensity of her grief, it would still leave a deep and lasting impression, and that her whole nature had been changed by it."

"Great afflictions and violent passions," replied Monsieur de Nemours, "do greatly alter people; as for me, I am entirely changed since I returned from Flanders. Many persons have noticed this alteration, and even the dauphiness spoke of it last evening."

"It is true," said Madame de Clèves, "that she has noticed it, and I think I have heard her say something about it."

"I am not sorry, Madame," Monsieur de Nemours continued, "that she perceived it, but I should prefer that she should not be the only one to notice it. There are persons to whom one does not dare to give any other marks of the love one feels for them than those which do not affect them in any but an indirect way; and since one does not dare to show one's love, one would at least desire that they should see that one wishes not to be loved by any one else. One would like to have them know that there is no beauty, of whatever rank, whom one would not regard with indifference, and that there is no crown which one would wish to buy at the price of never seeing them. Women generally judge the love one has for them," he went on, "by the pains one takes to please them and to pursue them; but that is an easy matter, provided they are charming. What is difficult is not to yield to the pleasure of pursuing them,— it is to avoid them, from fear of showing to the public or to them one's feelings; and the most distinctive mark of a true attachment is to become entirely different from what one was, to be indifferent to ambition or pleasure after having devoted one's whole life to one or the other."

Madame de Clèves readily understood the reference to her in these words. It seemed to her that she ought to answer them and express her disapproval; it also seemed to her that she ought not to listen to them or show that she took his remarks to herself: she believed that she ought to speak, and also that she ought to say nothing. The remarks of Monsieur de Nemours pleased and offended her equally; she saw in them a confirmation of what the crown princess had made her think,—she found them full of gallantry and respect, but also bold and only too clear. Her interest in the prince caused

an agitation which she could not control.
The vaguest words of a man one likes produce more emotion than the open declarations of a man one does not like. Hence she sat without saying a word, and Monsieur de Nemours noticed her silence, which would have seemed to him a happy omen, if the arrival of Monsieur de Clèves had not put an end to the talk and to his visit.

The Prince de Clèves had come to tell his wife the latest news about Sancerre; but she had no great curiosity about the rest of that affair. She was so interested in what had just happened that she could hardly hide her inattention. When she was able to think it all over, she perceived that she had been mistaken when she fancied that she had become indifferent to Monsieur de Nemours. His words had made all the impression he could desire, and had thoroughly convinced her of his passion. His actions harmonized too well with his words for her to have any further doubts on the subject. She did not any longer indulge in the hope of not loving him; she merely determined to give him no further sign of it. This was a difficult undertaking,—how difficult she knew already. She was aware that her only chance of success lay in avoiding the prince, and her mourning enabled her to live in retirement; she made it a pretext for not going to places where she might meet him. She was in great dejection; her mother's death appeared to be the cause, and she sought no other.

Monsieur de Nemours was in despair at not seeing her oftener; and knowing that he should not meet her at any assembly or entertainment at which the whole court was present, he could not make up his mind to go to them; he pretended a great interest in hunting, and made up hunting-parties on the days of the queens' assemblies. For a long time a slight indisposition served as a pretext for staying at home, and thus escaping going to places where he knew that Madame de Clèves would not be.

Monsieur de Clèves was ailing at nearly the same time, and Madame de Clèves never left his room during his illness; but when he was better and began to see company, and among others Monsieur de Nemours, who, under the pretext of being still weak, used to spend a good part of every day with him, she determined not to stay there. Nevertheless, she could not make up her mind to leave during his first visits; it was so long since she had seen him that she was anxious to meet him again. He too managed to make her listen to him, by what seemed like general talk; though she understood, from its reference to what he had said in his previous visit to her, that he went hunting to get an opportunity for meditation, and that he stayed away from the assemblies because she was not there.

At last Madame de Clèves put into execution her decision to leave her husband's room when the duke should be there, though she found it a difficult task. Monsieur de Nemours observed that she avoided him, and was much pained.

Monsieur de Clèves did not at first notice his wife's conduct; but at last he saw that she was unwilling to stay in his room when company was present. He spoke to her about it, and she replied that she did not think it quite proper that she should meet every evening all the young men of the court. She begged him to let her lead a more retired life than she had done before, because the presence of her mother, who was renowned for her virtue, had authorized many things impossible for a woman of her age.

Monsieur de Clèves, who was generally kind and pleasant to his wife, was not so on this occasion; he told her he was averse to any change in her conduct. She was tempted to tell him that there was a report that Monsieur de Nemours was in love with her; but she did not feel able to mention his name. She was also ashamed to assign a false reason, and to hide the truth from a man who had so good an opinion of her.

A few days later, the king happened to be with the queen when she was receiving, and the company was talking about horoscopes and predictions. Opinions were divided about the credence that ought to be given to them. The queen was inclined to believe in them; she maintained that after so many predictions had come true, it was impossible to doubt the exactness of this science. Others again held that the small number of lucky hits out of the numerous predictions that were made, proved that they were merely the result of chance.

"In former times," said the king, "I was very curious about the future; but I was told so much that was false or improbable that I became convinced that we can know nothing certain. A few years ago a famous astrologer came here. Every one went to see him, I as well as the rest, but without saying who I was; and I carried with me Monsieur de Guise and D'Escars, sending them into the room in front of me. Nevertheless the astrologer addressed me first, as if he thought I was their master; perhaps he knew me, although he said something to me which seemed to show that he did not know who I was. He prophesied that I should be killed in a duel; then he told Monsieur de Guise that he would be killed from behind, and D'Escars that he would have his skull broken by a kick from a horse. Monsieur de Guise was almost angry at hearing this, — as if he were accused of running away; D'Escars was no more pleased at learning that he was going to perish by such an unfortunate accident, — so that we all left the astrologer in extreme discontent. I have no idea what will happen to Monsieur de Guise or to D'Escars, but it is very unlikely that I shall be killed in a duel. The King of Spain and I have just made peace; and even if we had not, I doubt if we should resort to a personal combat, and it seems unlikely that I should challenge him, as my father challenged Charles V."

After the king had mentioned the unhappy end which had been foretold him, those who had supported astrology gave up and agreed that it was unworthy of belief. "For my part," said Monsieur de Nemours, "I am the last man in the world to place any confidence in it;" and turning to Madame de Clèves, near whom he was, he said in a low voice: "I was told that I should be made happy by the kindness of the woman for whom I should have the most violent and the most respectful passion. You may judge, Madame, whether I ought to believe in predictions."

The dauphiness, who fancied, from what Monsieur de Nemours had said aloud, that he was mentioning some absurd prophecy that had been made about him, asked him what he was saying to Madame de Clèves.

He would have been embarrassed by this question if he had had less presence of mind; but he answered without hesitation: "I was saying, Madame, that it had been predicted about me that I should rise to a lofty position to which I should not even dare to aspire."

"If that is the only prediction that has been made about you," replied the dauphiness, smiling, and thinking of the English scheme, "I do not advise you to denounce astrology; you might find good reasons for supporting it."

Madame de Clèves understood what the crown princess referred to; but she also understood that the happiness of which Monsieur de Nemours spoke, was not that of being king of England.

As it was some time since her mother's death, Madame de Clèves had to appear again in society and to resume her visits at court. She met Monsieur de Nemours at the dauphiness's and at her own house, whither he often came with young nobles of his own age, in order not to be talked about; but she never saw him without an agitation which he readily perceived.

In spite of the care she took to escape his glances and to talk less with him than with others, certain things inadvertently escaped her which convinced this prince that she was not indifferent to him. A less observant man than he would not, perhaps, have noticed them; but so many women had been in love with him that it was hard for him not to know when he was loved. He perceived that the Chevalier de Guise was his rival, and that prince knew that Monsieur de Nemours was his. He was the only man at court who would have discovered this truth; his interest had rendered him more clear-sighted than the others. The knowledge they had of each other's feelings so embittered their relations that although there was no open breach, they were opposed in everything. In running at the ring and in all the amusements in which the king took part they were always on different sides, and their rivalry was too intense to be hidden.

The English scheme often recurred to Madame de Clèves, and she felt that Monsieur de Nemours would not be able to withstand the king's advice and Lignerolles' urging. She noticed with pain that this last had not yet returned, and she awaited him with impatience. If she had followed his movements, she would have learned the condition of that matter; but the same feeling that inspired her curiosity compelled her to conceal it, and she contented herself with making inquiries about the beauty, intelligence, and character of Queen Elizabeth. A portrait of her was carried to the palace, and she found Elizabeth more beautiful than was pleasant to her, and she could not refrain from saying that it must flatter her.

"I don't think so," replied the dauphiness, who was present. "Elizabeth has a great reputation as a beauty and as the possessor of a mind far above the common, and I know that all my life she has been held up to me as an example. She ought to be attractive if she is like Anne Boleyn, her mother. Never was there a more amiable woman or one more charming both in appearance and disposition. I have been told that her face was exceptionally vivacious, and that she in no way resembled most English beauties."

"It seems to me," said Madame de Clèves, "that I have heard that she was born in France."

"Those who think so," replied the crown princess, are in error, "and I will tell you her history in a few words. She was born of a good English family. Henry VIII. had been in love with her sister and her mother, and it had even been suspected that she was his daughter. She came here with the sister of Henry VII., who married Louis XII. This young and gallant princess found it very hard to leave the court of France after her husband's death; but Anne Boleyn, who shared her mistress's feelings, decided to stay. The late king was in love with her, and she remained as maid of honor to Queen Claude. This queen died, and Madame Marguerite, the king's sister, the Duchess of Alençon, since then Queen of Navarre, whose stories you have seen, added Anne to her suite; it was from her that this queen received her inclination toward the new religion. Then Anne returned to England, where she delighted every one. She had French manners, which please all nations; she sang well, and danced charmingly. She was made a lady in waiting to Queen Catherine of Aragon, and King Henry VIII. fell desperately in love with her.

"Cardinal Wolsey, his favorite and prime minister, desired to be made pope; and being dissatisfied with the emperor for not supporting his claims, he resolved to avenge himself by allying the king his master with

France. He suggested to Henry VIII. that his marriage with the emperor's aunt was null and void, and proposed to him to marry the Duchess of Alençon, whose husband had just died. Anne Boleyn, being an ambitious woman, looked on this divorce as a possible step to the throne. She began to instil into the King of England the principles of Lutheranism, and persuaded the late king to urge at Rome Henry's divorce, in the hope of his marriage with Madame d'Alençon. Cardinal Wolsey contrived to be sent to France on other pretexts to arrange this affair; but his master would not consent to have the proposition made, and sent orders to Calais that this marriage was not to be mentioned.

"On his return from France, Cardinal Wolsey was received with honors equal to those paid to the king himself; never did a favorite display such haughtiness and vanity. He arranged an interview between the two kings, which took place at Boulogne. Francis I. offered his hand to Henry VIII., who was unwilling to take it; they treated each other with great splendor, each giving the other clothes like those he himself wore. I remember having heard that those the late king sent to the King of England were of crimson satin trimmed with pearls and diamonds arranged in triangles, the cloak of white velvet embroidered with gold. After spending a few days at Boulogne, they went to Calais. Anne Boleyn was quartered in the house with Henry VIII. in the queen's suite, and Francis I. made her the same presents and paid her the same honors as if she had been a queen herself. At last, after being in love with her for nine years, Henry married her, without waiting for the annulment of his first marriage, which he had long been asking of Rome. The pope at once excommunicated him; this so enraged Henry that he declared himself the head of the Church, and carried all England into the unhappy change of religion in which you now see it.

"Anne Boleyn did not long enjoy her grandeur, for one day, when she thought her position assured by the death of Catherine of Aragon, she happened to be present with all the court when the Viscount Rochford, her brother, was running at the ring. The king was suddenly overwhelmed by such an access of jealousy that he instantly left the spot, hastened to London, and gave orders for the arrest of the queen, the Viscount Rochford, and many others whom he believed to be the queen's lovers or confidants. Although this jealousy seemed the work of a moment, it had for some time been instigated by the Viscountess Rochford, who could not endure her husband's intimacy with the queen, and represented it to the king as criminal intimacy; consequently he, being already in love with Jane Seymour, thought only of getting rid of Anne Boleyn. In less than three weeks he succeeded in having the queen and her brother brought to trial and beheaded, and he married Jane

Seymour. He had afterward several wives, whom he either divorced or put to death, among others Catherine Howard, who had been the confidant of the Viscountess of Rochford, and was beheaded with her. Hence she was punished for the crimes with which she had blackened Anne Boleyn, and Henry VIII., having reached a monstrous size, died."

All the ladies present thanked the dauphiness for teaching them so much about the English court, and among others Madame de Clèves, who could not refrain from asking more questions about Queen Elizabeth.

The dauphiness had miniatures painted of all the beauties of the court to send to the queen her mother. The day when that of Madame de Clèves was receiving the last touches the crown princess came to spend the afternoon with her. Monsieur de Nemours was also there, for he neglected no opportunity of seeing Madame de Clèves, although he never seemed to court her so-

ciety. She was so beautiful that day that he would surely have fallen in love with her then if he had not done so already; but he did not dare to sit with his eyes fixed on her, while she feared lest he should show too plainly the pleasure he found in looking at her.

The crown princess asked Monsieur de Clèves for a miniature he had of his wife, to compare it with the one that was painting. All who were there expressed their opinion of both, and Madame de Clèves asked the painter to make a little correction in the hair of the old one. The artist took the miniature out of its case, and after working on it, set it down on the table.

For a long time Monsieur de Nemours had been desiring to have a portrait of Madame de Clèves. When he saw this one, though it belonged to her husband, whom he tenderly loved, he could not resist the temptation to steal it; he thought that among the many persons present he should not be suspected.

The dauphiness was seated on the bed, speaking low to Madame de Clèves, who was standing in front of her. One of the curtains was only partly closed, and Madame de Clèves was able to see Monsieur de Nemours, whose back was against the table at the foot of the bed, without turning his head pick up something from this table. She at once guessed that it was her portrait, and she was so embarrassed that the crown princess noticed she was not listening to her, and asked her what she was looking at. At these words Monsieur de Nemours turned round and met Madame de Clèves' eyes fastened on him; he felt sure that she must have seen what he had just done.

Madame de Clèves was greatly embarrassed. Her reason bade her ask for her portrait; but if she asked for it openly, she would announce to every one the prince's feelings for her, and by asking for it privately, she would give him an opportunity to speak to her of his love, so that at last she judged it better to let him keep it, — and she was very glad to be able to grant him a favor without his knowing that she did it of her own choice. Monsieur de Nemours, who observed her embarrassment and guessed its cause, came up to her and said in a low voice: "If you saw what I ventured to do, be good enough, Madame, to let me suppose that you know nothing about it; I do not dare to ask anything more." Then he went away, without waiting for an answer.

The dauphiness, accompanied by all her ladies, went out for a walk. Monsieur de Nemours locked himself up in his own room, being unable to contain his joy at having in his possession a portrait of Madame de Clèves. He felt all the happiness that love can give. He loved the most charming woman of the court, and felt that in spite of herself she loved him; he saw in everything she did the agitation and embarrassment which love evokes in the innocence of early youth.

That evening every one looked carefully for the portrait; when they found the case, no one supposed that it had been stolen, but that it had been dropped somewhere. Monsieur de Clèves was distressed at its loss, and after hunting for it in vain, told his wife, but evidently in jest, that she doubtless had some mysterious lover to whom she had given the portrait, or who had stolen it, for no one but a lover would care for the portrait without the case.

Although these words were not said seriously, they made a deep impression on the mind of Madame de Clèves and filled her with remorse. She thought of the violence of her love for Monsieur de Nemours, and perceived that she could not control either her words or her face. She reflected that Lignerolles had retunred, and that the English scheme had no terrors for her; that she had no longer grounds for suspecting the dauphiness; and finally, that, as she was without further defence, her only safety was in flight. Since, however, she knew she could not go away, she saw that she was in a most perilous condition, and ready to fall into what she judged to be the greatest possible misfortune, — namely, betraying to Monsieur de Nemours the interest she felt in him. She recalled everything her mother had said to her on her death-bed, and her advice to try everything rather than enter upon a love-affair. She remembered what her husband had said about her sincerity when he was speaking about Madame de Tournon, and it seemed to her that it was her duty to confess her passion for Monsieur de Nemours. She pondered over this for a long time; then she was astonished that the thought occurred to her: she deemed it madness, and fell **back** into **the agony of** indecision.

END OF VOL. I.

www.ingramcontent.com/pod-product-compliance
Lightning Source LLC
Chambersburg PA
CBHW020247170426
43202CB00008B/256